How to Write an IB History Essay:

The Safe Hands Approach

How to Write an IB History Essay:

The Safe Hands Approach

JOE THOMAS AND LORENZO BREWER

ZOUEV PUBLISHING

Published 2013

Printed by Lightning Source

ISBN 978-0-9560873-6-2, paperback.

"Even God cannot change the past."

Agathon

About the book:

How to write an IB History Essay: The Safe Hands Approach is for students studying IB History at either Higher or Standard Levels, at any point in the course. The Safe Hands Approach is a series of simple, effective techniques that are guaranteed to improve your essay writing. This book is all about skills and their application: it doesn't matter which period or topics you are studying, the principles outlined in the book will apply to you. The book is collaborative: a teacher explains the techniques and an IB student provides both insight as to how the approach helps and annotated sample work.

Your essay writing confidence and ability will improve if you adopt the Safe Hands Approach.

"The approach gives you a way of safely knowing that, given any question, you can write a solid, convincing, and ultimately successful IB History essay." (Lorenzo Brewer, IB History Student)

About the Authors:

Joe Thomas studied History at Oxford as an undergraduate and has spent the last thirteen years in education including almost a decade's worth of experience in the IB as teacher, coordinator and examiner. He has an MA in History from Oxford, an MA with distinction in English and Creative Writing, is a PhD researcher at the University of London, and runs an academic consultancy.

Lorenzo Brewer studied with Joe for eight months in the lead up to his IB examinations in 2013. He achieved a 7 in History at Higher Level.

Introduction

Who this book is for

IB History is too hard. We all know that. And there are reasons why. I'll explain them. And I'll explain how you can overcome them.

This book is for all IB History Students, Higher and Standard Levels, whether at the beginning of the course, the middle, desperately revising for final exams, or at any point in between. This is a book about essay writing skills: it doesn't matter which period or topics you are studying, the principles outlined in the book will apply to you. It is not necessary to be familiar with the historical content that I discuss to benefit from the techniques that I explain. Equally, while much of the discussion relates to Higher Level Paper 3 style questions, the principles hold true for Paper 2 and therefore Standard Level – and I explain why. There are annotated example essays from questions on both papers. Your essay writing confidence and ability will improve if you adopt the Safe Hands Approach: it will hold you in good stead for further academic study and even into your professional life. Knowing how to construct and support an argument, and doing it under immense pressure in an exam situation is a vital skill. This book will help you to achieve it.

The book was written with an IB student who achieved a 7 at Higher Level by following the approach. He has contributed comments in each chapter showing how it worked for him. The essays I examine at the end of each chapter are his, written as part of a revision programme in the months leading up to his exams. They are a little longer than you might be reasonably able to do in an exam, but again, the principles hold true and they were prepared as revision essays.

Here's what he has to say about the Safe Hands approach:

"When I first began working on history essays at IB Higher Level, I found myself confused and often frustrated. The demands on the teaching staff to cover the syllabus meant that there was 'never time' to focus on the problem of 'how' and 'why' we wrote essays. My essays were often far too long, contained extended sections of useless description and, sadly, failed to analytically answer the question I had been given.

"I think that this problem, common to many of my peers and students around the world, is at the core of this book; it doesn't just answer the 'how' of essay writing, but the 'why'.

"I gave in essay after essay, frustrated by the apparent absence of progress (I was always stuck on 11), and never felt like I knew what to do to get better. The tools to improve, the step-by-step changes I needed to make, were the key elements that make up the approach. The security it gave me allowed me to go on and write with confidence and my grades improved quickly.

"Through the Safe Hands approach I began to realize that, by writing using the approach, the information at your disposal is moulded into an analytical structure. The approach gives you a way of safely knowing that, given any question, you can write a solid, convincing, and ultimately successful IB History essay.

"The Safe Hands approach also allows you to detach yourself from the trap of drowning in information: the sheer size of the syllabus means that its easy to become obsessed with assimilating as much as possible. Working with the Safe Hands approach forces you to prioritize and synthesize that information, encouraging instead its successful application.

I hope that using this book, the approach is as rewarding and as useful for you as it was for me."

Why I've written this book

I love teaching IB History. (Really. Even when a student tricked me into thinking Sergio Busquets was a Nationalist General in the Spanish Civil War. He is the holding midfielder for Barcelona.) It is a wonderful subject and prepares students incredibly well for the demands of Higher Education and professional life. The underpinning principles of assimilation, analysis and articulation are vital and worthy. History provides an opportunity to reflect, think, and write with conviction and flair. The skills that students learn in IB History will set them up for the rest of their lives. I owe everything I have achieved to my History lessons at school. Arguably, that's not much, of course, but I do like to think that I am not a complacent person (lazy, perhaps, but not complacent) and the scrutiny I bring to things in my everyday life is down to the study of history. If nothing else, applying yourself in history lessons will enable you to discuss interesting things with interesting people at dinner parties when you are older, and this is a valuable skill.

But IB History is very, very tough: I am sympathetic to your plight.

This introduction explains why, and the guide itself will offer an approach to counter the problems outlined in the introduction. I will explain the key elements needed to craft a decent essay and will take a close look at sample responses written by a student who followed these principles with me over a period of six months.

This guide gets to the heart of what makes a good History essay despite, not because of, the difficulties associated with the syllabus, the mark schemes and the IB's lofty expectations. You will have a firm idea of how an essay can be shaped, organised and expressed in a way that gives the examiners no choice but to award you a high mark. It is the 'Safe Hands' approach: right from the first word of the essay, the reader will feel in 'Safe Hands', aware that the writer knows what she is doing, why, and that she is executing it efficiently. Examiners, above all (and I know, I am one – see? an achievement) like to nod and tick: to feel in safe hands.

The Problem

The IB History Higher Level Syllabus is ridiculous. It's brilliant, yes, but it is far too broad and demands far too much in terms of content. Students are asked to study and understand vast periods of History in considerable depth. When students ask: 'How can I improve my essays?' teachers are reduced to saying: 'more analysis, more depth, more historiography, more allusion, more facts, more argument. Oh, and do it in fewer words.' This is partly the fault of the mark schemes, partly the incomprehensible grade boundary decisions made each year after the exams, and partly the sheer size of the syllabus.

The mark schemes are problematic in Papers 2 and 3. There are superficial differences drawn between the two papers – we are told that Paper 2 is a thematic exercise and that Paper 3 is a deeper study. However, any good essay will draw on both of these elements. A Paper 2 essay without depth will be no more effective than a Paper 3 essay with no thematic understanding. Words and phrases are thrown around haphazardly: 'evaluation', 'synthesis' and 'interpretation, 'knowledge', 'critical commentary' and 'conceptual ability'. All of these are important skills and crucial in the production of a good essay, but the mark schemes do not make the differences in the concepts clear enough.

Equally, what is the difference between Papers 2 and 3? The mark schemes, in terms of the content of the Upper Mark Bands, are identical. The basic requirements are the same. And yet, for Paper 2, the highest mark band is 16-20 and for Paper 3 18-20. All good IB examiners will point out that in the Paper 3 mark scheme there are the italicized aspects, one of which you need to include for the very highest marks. These include 'conceptual ability' and understanding of why interpretations may differ from historian to historian. Does this mean that you have to perform better in a Paper 3 essay (i.e. include more sophisticated and more difficult techniques) to achieve 18 than you do in a Paper 2 essay for the same mark? It appears so. At an IB workshop I was informed that Paper 2 is more thematic and that Paper 3 is more specific. This is reductive and a fairly worthless distinction. If you follow my approach, the distinction becomes irrelevant – a good essay is a good essay. Ignore the mark schemes in terms of guidance, as they do not offer clarity on how the key requirements are to be achieved. I will show you how they match up to the Safe Hands approach.

Of course, this clarity I mention should, rightly, come from the teacher. And here lies the second problem: the grade boundaries are such that the upper mark range becomes almost entirely incidental. In a subject where 14/20 will achieve a 7, it is very, very rare for students to score much higher. Examiners are too scared to award marks at the highest levels. How many of you have actually achieved more than 16 from your teachers in an exam essay? And how many of you, when asking what you have to do to get 17-20, have simply been told that 16 is a 7 and not to worry about it? I know I have been guilty of this as a teacher myself. By making the top mark bands basically irrelevant for the majority of students – many of whom are immensely talented – the IB has confused the issue of what makes an effective essay. They appear to be saying: 'get 14/20 and you're doing very well. Our subject is too hard to do any better and you're foolish to want to try.' This does not encourage ambitious students and it frustrates teachers who want to do exactly that.

The third issue is syllabus content. Long ago, when the syllabus changed, I spoke to a Senior examiner offering an idea: keep Papers 1 and 2 as they are but reduce Paper 3 to one topic instead of three. Make the Paper 3 exam two essays in two hours. That way, the students will have the time to study, say, Russia from 1853-1924 in depth and will also be able to develop their critical and evaluative skills while doing so.

Think about it. In that period in Russia, a quite extraordinary amount happened. A class could spend a year studying the Revolutions alone. Or Alexander II's reforms. Or the impact of the war. Or Lenin's Russia. Yet, the IB thinks the whole lot can be done in a couple of months. This enormous amount of content means that teachers are rushing to finish the syllabus in time and struggle to focus at all on the skills needed to assimilate, analyse and articulate the information they are throwing at the students, desperate to avoid accusations of not fulfilling all the board's requirements. How many of your teachers have said to you: 'Yeah, we won't bother with that part and just hope other questions will come up that you can answer.' I've done it myself.

It is an impossible job to prepare for everything you are, according to the syllabus, supposed to do.

Recently, I sat down with a student who has worked incredibly hard and covered approximately 90% of the entire syllabus. Even then, looking at past papers, it was impossible to guarantee that he could answer what he needed to, as the questions cover so much ground. Put simply: there is too much stuff to know! I firmly believe that the IB has sacrificed its commitment to skills in favour of content in the HL History syllabus.

With the sheer breadth of the syllabus, and the consequence that there is little time in class left to actually discuss the subject and evaluate historical interpretation, exam essays become even harder.

How do you combine depth of knowledge, pertinent, considered analysis and a keen appreciation of historical debate in only 45/50 minutes?

I'm going to show you. It's called The Safe Hands approach. And it works for Paper 2 and Paper 3, so don't worry about the content or the questions. Just assimilate the skills and practice. A lot.

Contents

1. The thesis and challenging the question

'The problems of Dual Power led to the end of the Provisional Government.' Do you agree?

2. The thematic structure

'The assassination of Alexander II indicates that his rule was ultimately conservative.' To what extent do you agree with this statement?

3. The difference between narration and analysis

'The Duma system was purely a means of maintaining power.' Discuss this statement with reference to Nicholas II up to 1914

4. The use of evidence

Compare and contrast the nature of the two revolutions in 1917

5. The importance of historiography

'The nature of Tsarist rule from 1881-1914 was dominated by a balancing act of liberal need and autocratic desire.' Assess the validity of this statement

6. The allusive style and the benefits of counterfactual thinking

'Lenin's ultimate goal was the creation of a single-party Bolshevik state.' Assess the validity of this statement

7. A word on Paper Two

Chapter One – The thesis and challenging the question

"I used to really struggle with introductions, giving all my essays a lack of direction, and worse, a sense that I was scared or insecure about my own ability to deal with the historical situations being discussed. I think that this is an immediate red flag to any reader, and this sense of insecurity and fear will only lead to a sense of unease, which detracts from the argument being made.

"Using the three-sentence structure however, provides you with a simple and effective way of staying focused on the historical material, demonstrate the awareness that gives the reader the sense that the essay will go on to be effective and analytical, and finally, ensure for yourself that you have a sense of direction. Although the introduction by no means dictates the quality of the essay, it is (for me at least), the place where you as a writer gain the confidence to unravel a well thought out argument.

"My introductions were the first thing that improved as I began to apply the methodology outlined in the book; the change made a huge difference to the way that my essays were constructed and how they felt as analytical pieces of writing."

It's a myth that the introduction is **the most important part** of your essay. It's a bit like saying the words are the most important part of your essay. If you only write an introduction, you are going to get very few marks, no matter how good it is.

However, the introduction is a **fundamental part** of an essay and a strong introduction using the three-sentence structure is key to the Safe Hands approach.

Let me explain why.

An examiner does not have a great deal of time to scrutinise essays. This is not to say that he does not examine them carefully and award fair marks, but it does mean that he will make a judgement as to the overall quality of an essay based on the first thing he reads – the introduction. A weak introduction will not necessarily mean a low mark, just as a strong one won't guarantee a high mark. But the introduction sets the tone and the quality of the essay to come. Essentially, in an introduction, a student announces himself and is able to tell the examiner the following three things:

1) I understand the question
2) I have recognised and considered the implications of the question

3) I have identified the best approach to answering the question and imposed my own analytical structure

If the examiner sees these qualities in an introduction, then he will read on confidently, ticking and nodding, aware that the main body of the essay relates back to the introduction and structure related in it. He feels in safe hands, that the student is in control and knows what he is doing.

Essays are three parts, ultimately – say what you're going to say (introduction), say it (main body), say it again (conclusion). Going by that very general principle, your introduction should cover absolutely everything you are going to say in your whole essay. That may sound daunting, but it shouldn't. It's about offering breadth and depth in your expression.

Let me show you an example.

An effective introduction in an exam essay need have only three sentences, which set up your thesis and structure. We'll use the following question to illustrate the principle –

'The problems of Dual Power led to the end of the Provisional Government.' Do you agree?

<u>Sentence one</u> should demonstrate a broad understanding of the demands of the question. In this case, a simple first sentence will state that the Provisional Government did indeed have problems. A more sophisticated answer would begin with some identification of what those problems were, in broad terms, **not** a specific list. E.g.:

The "problems" of Dual Power were twofold: not only were they, as is implied by the question, a set of difficulties the government encountered while in power, but were also the fundamental ideological paradox which underlay it.

The quality in this first sentence is that the student shows to the examiner that he will consider both the specific problems of the

16

Provisional Government – the question of foreign loans, the problems of war, domestic economic failure etc – and also the fundamental issue that lay at the heart of Dual Power. In other words, the student demonstrates he will discuss specific evidence while maintaining a broad political, ideological and conceptual perspective. The suggestion from this opening sentence is that the student has the *potential* as the mark scheme states, to hit the key areas.

Marks 18-20:

In-depth and accurate historical knowledge is applied consistently and convincingly to support critical commentary. In addition answers may reveal a high level of conceptual ability. **(Diploma Programme History Guide, 2008. Subsequent references are to this edition.)**

The 'set of difficulties' referenced in the opening line relates to 'in-depth and accurate historical knowledge' while the identification of the 'fundamental ideological paradox' provides the 'high level of

17

conceptual ability'. Of course, the student needs to go and do this in the main body, but with this opening sentence, an examiner will already be thinking that he will do.

Sentence two should develop the connection between the broad ideas of sentence one and the question itself. Additionally, in this sentence, there is an opportunity to 'challenge' the question. This is an idea I want to expand on briefly.

The concept of challenging the question is a controversial one. While the IB place 'risk-taking' in their Learner Profile, the reality is that to achieve a high mark in a History essay, you need to cover all the basics before attempting any potentially dangerous analysis or ideas. Now, why should an idea of your own be dangerous? The reason is sad, but simple: it is impossible for an IB student to come up with a valid thesis that hasn't already been proposed, discussed and scrutinised by professional historians. History examiners are well versed in Historical debate and no doubt will prefer certain schools of thought to others. Equally, an examiner wants to see an inquiring mind in an essay, one that demonstrates awareness but is not necessarily foolish enough to nail his colours to the mast. Because making a statement in the introduction that defines an argument reductively *is* foolish. Much better to show that there are *implications* to a question. By this I mean there are elements to the debate that may not be clear-cut. The importance is balance – it is too early to show the examiner that you fall on either side. Better to demonstrate awareness of the debate. In this case, being bold is not especially wise. You run the very real, life-changing low-grade-and-university-place-related risk of alienating the examiner in the very first paragraph. So, the next time your teacher suggests you challenge the question, instead of blithely criticising it or showing a definite preference for a particular school of thought – i.e. instead of taking a risk – show that you realise that there are *issues* with a question in terms of interpretation and analysis.

(I suppose that the IB Learner Profile meaning of 'risk' is essentially different to our daily conception of it, e.g. gambling, running across a busy road or asking someone out on a date. Really, I think it means, in IB terms, being brave and considered in your choices and defending your position with conviction and balance. Which isn't really a risk, if you think about it. Doing that should get you good marks.)

Here is an example of how to achieve all this, based on the same question, following on from the previous example sentence.

It was the problem of Dual Power though, that really brought about the Provisional Government's downfall – the ideological hedonism of many of the members; one could not exist while the other prevailed, and yet members of both the Soviet and the Provisional Government were uncompromisingly tied to each other.

The student here recognises that while there were specific difficulties, ultimately with the fundamental issue of Dual Power, these difficulties could not be overcome. He identifies a concept – 'ideological hedonism' –, which is both pertinent and perceptive. And he shows the examiner that he understands the sense of confusion and brinkmanship within the Dual Power. In other words, the political system was flawed to an extent that any attempt to address specific problems by the Provisional Government was scuppered by a reliance on the Soviet. This explanation develops the first sentence by revealing an understanding of what the question is getting at – that the broader issues of the political system are worthy of analysis as much as the problems Russia faced in 1917. The student is outlining his thesis over these two sentences: firstly, that there were political and economic decisions that had to be made, and secondly, that these decisions were undermined by the relationship between the Provisional Government and the Soviet. Again, this sentence demonstrates the potential for the essay to score highly.

Events are placed in the historical context. There is a clear understanding of historical processes and (where appropriate) comparison and contrast.

By referring to 'ideological hedonism' and the idea that 'one could not exist while the other prevailed' the student shows a keen understanding of both immediate context and the broader question of historical process and causation.

Sentence three should set up the structure of the essay. In the next chapter I will deal more closely with the best way to structure an essay. In that sense, the first two chapters should be read together in terms of writing an effective introduction. Essentially though, the sentence should map out the areas you will write about and cover everything so that the examiner immediately understands where your argument is heading. If this is achieved, the examiner is able then to simply go through the essay nodding and ticking at all the appropriate evidence and ideas that you use. The point is that with a careful third sentence explaining the key areas for discussion, the content that then supports your thesis will feel inevitable for the examiner. He will feel, once again, as if he is in Safe Hands.

Here is the final sentence of the introduction we have been working on.

Three key periods characterized the Provisional government's downfall: its post-February 1917 formation and ideological formation, Bolshevik agitation and the July days, and Kerensky and the Bolshevik Coup D'état.

This sentence covers all of the areas needed to properly answer the question and in broad terms covers everything that will be written about. The examiner sees that the student will focus on how the

Provisional Government was formed, what the Bolsheviks did to exacerbate the problems of 1917, and the final end to the Provisional Government in the October Revolution, cleverly described here as the 'Bolshevik Coup D'état. (This shows an understanding that the October Revolution was not a popular movement as such, but representative of Lenin's idea that his party were the vanguard of the proletariat. This short phrase reveals a high level of conceptual understanding.)

In terms of the mark scheme, this third sentence will also potentially score highly.

Answers are well structured and clearly expressed, using evidence to support relevant, balanced and well-focused arguments. Synthesis is highly developed, with knowledge and critical commentary fully and effectively integrated.

By including the 'three key periods' and showing that each of these periods was marked by both specific events (e.g. 'the July Days') and underlying ideological issues (e.g. 'Bolshevik Coup D'état) the student further develops his thesis and shows how he will measure the importance of the core problem of Dual Power against the specific challenges that the Provisional Government faced. He outlines a three-part structure and shows there is considerable room for synthesis and critical commentary.

By following this three-sentence introduction strategy, you leave the examiner feeling confident in your ability to identify and analyse the essential evidence needed to effectively answer the question.

Let's now have a look at the whole essay and how the thesis and introduction is sustained.

'The problems of Dual Power lead to the end of the Provisional Government.' Do you agree?

The "problems" of Dual Power were twofold: not only were they, as is implied by the question, a set of difficulties the government encountered while in power; it was also a fundamental ideological paradox, which underlay it. It was the problem of Dual Power though, that really brought about the Provisional Government's downfall – the ideological hedonism [*High level of conceptual thinking*] of many of the members; one could not exist while the other prevailed, and yet members of both the Soviet and the

Provisional Government were uncompromisingly tied to each other. Three key periods characterized the Provisional government's downfall: Its post-February 1917 formation and ideological formation, Bolshevik agitation and the July days, and Kerensky and the Bolshevik Coup D'état. [*Thematic/chronological structure – though I would employ a more directly thematic approach*]

The establishment of the Dual Power itself was an ideological paradox [*Conceptual thinking*] that both the Provisional Government and the Soviet would never fully recover from. [*Thesis – links to the introduction*] It haunted it early in its post-February revolution days: it was a government made in the salons that had emerged from a revolution made in the streets. [*'Anecdotal' evidence – adds colour*] The formation of the provisional government and dual power in March of 1917 was in part due to Soviet's leaders' own inexperience in the true matters of state: it was more convenient for leaders like Chzheidze and later Tsraeteli to allow prince Lvov in to be in power, as it was his class that had run Russia for the past century. This meant that the Soviet seemed, to the Russian people at least; to have rejected its rightful place in power, while the Provisional government, totally illegitimate, live with it in tandem. This was compounded by the provisional governments stalling on the election of the Constituent Assembly; [*Political evidence*] although probably only due to Lvov desire for a government to "crown" the Russian revolution, the inability to form a government highlighted again one of the fundamental flaws that would lead to the dual power's eventual downfall. Both bodies acted together, but by not acting in a "revolutionary way" they confirmed fears in the post-February Petrograd streets that the government had fallen into the hands of the "counter-revolutionaries", and left it susceptible to Bolshevik agitation. [*Demonstrates flaws not just of the Dual Power but of the political situation in 1917 – and examines consequences that led to Bolshevik Coup*]

25

The July days were a product of the reluctance of the Dual Power's leaders to address its own ideological failings, this led to an armed revolution that would demonstrate the governments weakness, and set the stage for its eventual overthrow. [*Establishes paragraph thesis and links to introduction*] On the 18th of June 1917, the Soviet staged a rally of "revolutionary unity": it was intended to be a supporting cry for its continued participation in the provisional government. That the Bolsheviks marched too, under the banner of "All Power to the Soviet!" was even more telling: the mood in Russia was anti-provisional government, and it was clear with developments in the Stockholm peace conference in May that the Russian's were not going to be getting out of the First World War soon. [*Excellent use of evidence – the selection adds an analytical element*] The combination of the Bolshevik's exploitation of the Dual Power's fundamental ideological flaws, and its inability to take decisive action in the war caused a mass uprising in July. On Tuesday the 4th of July, some 50,000 angry men, many of them soldiers from the Krondstadt naval base, surrounded the Tauride Palace demanding for soviet seizure of power. Chernov was sent out to calm the crowd, but was bundled into a car and only saved by the passionate words of Trotsky. The feelings of the Russian people were summed up by worker who grabbed the SR leader: "take power, you son of a bitch, when its handed to you!" [*Perceptive and adds colour*] The July days proved that there was an overwhelming democratic rejection of the dual power system; Russia's own proletariat had openly begged for the Soviet to take power. Yet the Soviet's leaders were not prepared to acknowledge it, and dismissed it as "Bolshevik demagogy". This is a moment perhaps, where the nature of the Dual Power system itself was compounded by the ideological disposition of its leaders: Tsraeteli and others believed that the "bourgeois phase" of the revolution had to happen, and were not willing to break from a traditionally Marxist framework. They were convinced that the creation of a new coalition would save the Dual Power, ignoring the ideological paradox that underlay it.

26

In reality it was only Lenin's reluctance to sanction the July Days uprising, perhaps because of his sense that some of the army still supported the Provisional Government, which had saved it. [*Excellent conclusion to the paragraph, which covers a considerable amount of detail with effective critical commentary*]

Alexander Kerensky's addressing of the fundamental problem of Dual Power, [*Links to thesis as stated in introduction*] would, ironically, bring about the provisional government's end through a Bolshevik coup d'état that confirmed the paradox that underlay it. [*Identifies ultimate cause of failure of PG and shows conceptual thinking*] After the July Days uprising, Kerensky was seen by Lvov as the only man capable of rebuilding the provisional government. An extreme narcissist who fetishized Napoleonic imagery and dress, Kerensky saw himself as the saviour of the revolution. His first move as leader was to expel the soviets on the 18th of July (the same day his new provisional government moved into the Winter Palace) to the Smolny Institute, an old school for the nobility's daughters on the outskirts of Petrograd. Kerensky it seemed, believed that the Dual system was implausible; unsurprising, considering his own self-imposed destiny to save the revolution. Kerensky signalled thus the rejection of the soviet movement, compounding a series of conservative and repressive reforms both at home and at the front. Set in motion on the 8th of July, these would sow the seeds of a Bolshevik revolution based almost entirely on the premise that the provisional government was now in the hands of the "counter-revolutionaries", "industrialists" and "war mongers". Unlike the July Days, this new government did not have the express support of the soviet; the ideological hedonism that had characterized its actions had all but dissipated with its exile. After a series of unsuccessful attempts to push soviet soldiers at the front and the disastrous "Kornilov affair", the provisional government was left open to criticism by Lenin and the Bolshevik party who would argue that it had

27

become a "naked military dictatorship struggling for power". [*Demonstrates causal connections*] Both combined at the Moscow conference, a desperate attempt by Kerensky to rally moderate support, to confirm to any onlookers that Russia was still deeply divided between left and right: Sergei Semenov attended the conference and noted that the seating arrangements reflected Russia social divisions; it seemed that Kerensky had failed to unite the revolution and that the problems that had plague Dual power, would also undermine his power. On the 25th of October, the Bolsheviks would organize and carry out a revolution that would mark the end of the provisional government. Kerensky had rejected Dual Power because of its flaws; now those problems would bring about a broken, unpopular government's end. It was no surprise that in the pouring rain the Bolsheviks almost strolled into the Winter Palace to take power: The Dual Power, the provisional government and Kerensky were all already buried. [*Nice stylistic approach – combining anecdote with analysis*]

In conclusion, the nature of Dual Power itself, and the Dual Power's reluctance to address this problem lead to its eventual downfall. From its inception, the reality of the middle class liberalism of the provisional government could never function well with the raw revolutionary sentiment of the Soviet. [*Excellent summary*] The July Days demonstrated however, that the Soviet's leaders could not bring themselves to break with conventional Marxist revolutionary framework, even when the proletariat themselves demanded ideological malleability. This inability to compromise eventually brought about the Soviet's exile by Kerensky who did understand that the system could not function in its current form, but underestimated the ideological implication of his rejection. These three moments compounded to allow by the Bolshevik party, for the constant erosion of the Provisional Government's power until its final collapse on the 25th of October 1917. [*Lacks appreciation of historiography, throughout the essay*]

28

Chapter Two – The thematic structure

"Before regularly employing the thematic structure principle as part of my writing for IB History, I would often choose singular events, attempting to use them to explain the outcome of a historical situation. This however, immediately created a limitation in my essays: without addressing the wider historical currents that shaped particular situations, the quality of analysis was often lacking. Worse, my essays didn't give a sense that there was an understanding of the wider historical issues, contexts, or even that events co-existed as part of the wider issues that underpin any society.

"These wider issues are the foundation for the thematic structure. It provides immediately an indication that you understand that a combination of separate factors within a society, country, or time period affect a historical situation's outcome. Better still, the thematic structure provides this sense while also given you the freedom to judiciously synthesize and select the information which provides evidence for your argument, demonstrating an understanding of the multiplicity which shapes history.

"Finally, History essays at IB ultimately culminate in an exam, which demands quick thinking to create a feasible structure in which to develop an argument. The thematic structure provides this, given you a sense of security when approaching any essay, either at home or in an exam situation."

As explained in Chapter One, the introduction serves three purposes. The third is, arguably, the most significant – it needs to set up the structure for your essay. If an essay is a construction, then the three-part structure I have talked about are its foundations. Without a decent structure, your argument cannot flourish. Indeed, an essay's structure acts as an argument in itself: by identifying the key areas for consideration in the introduction, you are already demonstrating a keen eye for analysis. The very decision to divide the essay into component parts is an analytical one – it shows critical thinking and synthesis of ideas and evidence.

There are a number of ways to structure a History essay.

Perhaps the simplest and least sophisticated is to order it chronologically, to go through the relevant events and explain how they are connected to the question. The danger of this approach is that the essay becomes an exercise in narrative – the sheer descriptive weight of the essay disables any chance of genuine analysis. While the mark scheme talks of placing historical events in context – which will require a sense of narrative and chronology – by taking a solely chronological stance, it is nigh on impossible to show understanding of historical processes.

I understand 'historical processes' to refer to broad change in society and the reasons for this change: to, ultimately, show comprehension of causation be that on individual initiative, or for longer-term socio-economic-political reasons. Russia in 1917, for example, was dominated by individuals – Lvov, Kerensky, Lenin, Trotsky etc – but to attribute the dramatic changes of that year uniquely to individual decisions would discount the impact and shock of the removal of the traditional autocratic Tsarist system. Russia was (is) a vast country, and it can be overwhelming for a student to attempt to consider that the organs of power represent only a fraction of that country's opinion and desire.

Taking a chronological look at 1917 shows us the timeline of events that led eventually to the Bolshevik Coup, but it will not articulate the deeper societal tension that had been building for many years before. Chronology has its place, but a true understanding of causation is not a linear one. True, each 'historical event' has a singular uniqueness that means that if any event in the build up to the 'historical event' is changed in any way, then that singular uniqueness disappears – essentially, the Determinist position – and this is partly reliant on the chronological 'and then...' (And then this happened, and then this...etc). But an essay framed by an 'and then' structure will not take into account the multiplicity of factors that form an event's 'cause'. In mark scheme terms, a sound chronological structure may get you a 5, however the sophistication and synthesis needed for the higher marks is very unlikely.

So the question is, how to formulate a structure that is both pertinent to the question and also offers analytical and critical insight? The answer is to divide your response by theme or topic.

The Thematic Structure

Step One: the set-up

A thematic structure shows understanding of the multiplicity of causation. It enables the argument in an essay. It drives the examiner forward with more ticking and nodding. If we examiners learn in the first paragraph which three themes will be examined, each section will feel inevitable and considered. A thematic structure avoids problems associated with narrative, creates a framework for analysis, and assists in terms of employing supporting evidence, as each paragraph is like a mini essay in itself where evidence is collected under a specific heading.

Most history essays can be divided into three of a number of prevalent themes: Political, Economic, Social, Ideological, Military, etc. In reality, 90% of essays will be divided into Political, Economic and Social. Think of it this way: if a dictator has control over these three elements within a society, then his rule can be described as totalitarian. In other words, the Political, Economic and Social aspects of history are almost total. (The other themes I've mentioned can often be subsumed within these categories – e.g. Military may come under Political.)

In Chapter One we looked at an essay on Russia in 1917. I deliberately chose this example, as the structure, while appearing to have a chronological basis, is essentially thematic. Let's remind ourselves of the final sentence of the introduction:

Three key periods characterized the Provisional government's downfall: its post-February 1917 formation and ideological formation, Bolshevik agitation and the July days, and Kerensky and the Bolshevik Coup D'état.

Looking at the three sections outlined, the essay will focus on political, economic, ideological, and social factors. Arguably, the introduction would have been improved with a more direct proposition. 'The Provisional Government's downfall was due to a combination of political, economic and social factors.' However, by recognising the distinct periods, the student acknowledges the timescale of the question – a mere nine months.

Let's look at a different question to demonstrate the thematic structure even more clearly.

'The assassination of Alexander II indicates that his rule was ultimately conservative.' To what extent do you agree with this statement?

The question here is asking the student to assess the extent of Alexander's reforming tendency. It's a classic Alexander II question: was he the 'Tsar Liberator' or was he a conservative bent only on maintaining Tsarist authority? The historiography is fairly straightforward, and a decent line to take on such a question is that Alexander recognised the need for reform on an altruistic level, but also that if he failed to instigate change from above, in the context of 1848, forced change from below was a distinct possibility. Others suggest that while Alexander was indeed liberal, he was not quite liberal enough. These ideas are important in the formation of the thesis and the sense of challenging the question discussed in Chapter One.

How then to best evaluate the political achievements and philosophy of a leader? We need to measure his impact on Russia, and as I have indicated, that is most effective through an assessment of his influence on the political, social and economic aspects of society. By doing so, you show to the examiner that you understand that an overall judgement must be broken down into component parts for a clear and effective analysis to be made. This division is, as I have stated, an analysis in itself and is the first step to a critically impressive piece of writing.

Let's have a look at an introduction for this Alexander question.

Conservatism as an idea exists only in consideration to what other possible alternatives exist. To argue that Alexander II rule was "ultimately conservative" is to not consider what liberalizing reform meant in Russia, and how it was interpreted at different levels of society. Orlando Figes argues, in *Natasha's dance* that 1861 was a moment where Russian society became obsessed with its own national identity; the question becomes then, was Alexander II rule conservative in the popular or autocratic contexts? Was he conservative because of changing social tides, or because of policy? The question of conservatism is framed by a historiographical debate, which is examined in this essay by looking at social, political and economic changes.

This introduction shows an excellent appreciation of the intricacies of the question and considers the context of the time and the changes that the country underwent. I would suggest that bringing specific historiography this early into the essay is unnecessary and I might make one line clearer: I would clarify **Was he conservative because of changing social tides, or because of policy?** with a few words regarding the idea of change from above rather than below. In terms of structure though, the important element is that the student has shown us that the idea of conservatism can only be effectively examined if all aspects of society are addressed. Undoubtedly there was seismic change under Alexander II; the key is to perhaps demonstrate where the changes occurred, what the principal motivating force was, and how the Russian people were affected at all levels of society.

In terms of mark scheme, this introduction and structure provide the platform to achieve the following Assessment Objectives required for the top bands:

Assessment Objective 3: Synthesis and Evaluation

- *Evaluate different approaches to, and interpretations of, historical issues and events*

- *Develop critical commentary using the evidence base*
- *Synthesise by integrating evidence and critical commentary*

Assessment Objective 4: Use of Historical Skills

- *Demonstrate the ability to structure an essay, using evidence to support relevant, balanced and focused historical arguments*

The student has created the potential for this through his demonstration of an understanding of context and process, references to the historiography, an awareness of the implications of the question, and an indication of a structure that will allow for effective integration of evidence.

Step Two: sustaining the structure and argument

With a thematic structure, each section – in this case social, political and economic changes – becomes a mini essay in itself and therefore requires an introduction, or topic sentence, which will tie the paragraph back to the original thesis and clearly mark to the examiner the analytical progress and process of the essay. By defining each section in these terms, the examiner sees how your initial analysis has set up the critical evaluation of the rest of the essay. In other words, he knows what is coming and merely has to pick out the key bits of evidence and historiography that support the thesis.

Here are two of the topic sentences from our example essay:

1. The emancipation of the serfs, the most radical of Alexander II's social reforms, is representative of the ambiguous definitions of "liberal" that existed when Alexander took power in 1855.

2. Politically, Alexander's reforms demonstrated that he was willing to go down a cautious road, not matched by a new political generation, which Dominic Moon described as full of "intellectual nihilism".

Each of these sentences places the examiner squarely within the thesis and context of the argument. In the first, 'social reforms' indicates the theme; 'ambiguous definitions of liberal' shows the implications of the question and a high level of conceptual interpretation; and, 'the emancipation of the serfs, the most radical of Alexander II's social reforms' shows a keen eye for categorisation, recognising that while the emancipation was a political act, its impact was social.

In the second, Alexander's motivation and intention is raised and questioned in the context of a rising class of political agitators. Ultimately, this topic sentence shows an examiner that the student recognises the paradox at the heart of Alexander's reign: that he was a cautious reformer whose reform, however, was radical in many ways. From these topic sentences, the paragraphs now unfold with a synthesis of argument and development of the thesis, and the evidence to support it, evidence connected always to the topic: social, political or economic.

Let's now examine the entire essay.

'The assassination of Alexander II indicates that his rule was ultimately conservative.' To what extent do you agree with this statement?

Conservatism as an idea, exists only in consideration to what other possible alternatives exist. To argue that Alexander II rule was "ultimately conservative" is to not consider what liberalizing reform meant in Russia, and how it was interpreted at different levels of society. Orlando Figes argues, in *Natasha's dance* that 1861 was a moment where Russian society became obsessed with its own national identity; the question becomes then, was Alexander II rule conservative in the popular or autocratic contexts? [*Interesting approach to assessing the implications of the question: 'challenging' the question*] Was he conservative because of changing social tides, or because of policy? The question of conservatism is framed by a historiography debate, [*Indicates awareness of historical opinion*] which is examined in this essay by looking at social, political and economic changes. [*Thematic structure – clear and simple and showing historiography frame*]

The emancipation of the serfs, the most radical of Alexander II's social reforms, is representative of the ambiguous definitions of "liberal" that existed when Alexander took power in 1855. [*Links to thesis in introduction*] Russia's failure in the Crimean war had revealed her to be in many ways backwards, and this backwardness, especially in the treatment of Russia's peasant class, created a movement of middle class Russians who "sympathised" with the plight of the peasants. These were the sons and daughters of squires, old landowning men and women, who had mistreated Serf nannies. As part of the current of liberalism in Russia, they sought to absolve themselves of their "original sin", their guilt at the hundreds of years of suppression they had inflicted on the serfs: as Orlando Figes explains in Natasha's dance, 1855 was when "peasant question" became Russia's biggest social issue. [*Effective integration of historiography/evidence*] Indeed, Alexander's Edict of Emancipation in 1861, was as

41

much a reaction to genuine support of reform amongst middle class Russians as it was a reaction to maintain his autocratic power. [*Balanced analysis*]The reform may have finally "freed" some 23 million serfs, but there was also a high price to pay. Serfs now had debts they had to pay back to the state on "100% Mortgages" which had given them their land. Their cultivatable space went down by some 20% as noblemen kept the best land. The emancipation was indeed an extraordinary moment in Russian history, but it did not fulfil idealistic aims that had become part of Russian popular culture from 1855, or even the desires of the serfs themselves. People had hoped for a kind of self-sacrificial peasant love shown in Tolstoy's late story "The Master and the Man" [*Interesting contrast between statistical evidence and use of literature as social evidence*]; in essence, they did not feel as if emancipation had absolved them of their "original sin". This liberal desire however, could not be matched by the reality of dealing with an extraordinarily extensive state bureaucracy. The emancipation was a liberal reform, but Alexander's liberalism could not match popular support: his liberalism was the loosening of autocratic power, not its overhaul. Indeed W.E Moss describes the Tsar as "Cut off from his people", [*Further historiography effectively integrated*] and this was surely the problem that underlay liberal reform, Alexander was liberal, but not as liberal as his people.

Politically, Alexander's reforms demonstrated that he was willing to go down a cautious road, not matched by a new political generation which Dominic Moon described as full of "intellectual nihilism". [*Links well with the introduction and sets up paragraph thesis*] This was a generation of almost millenarian radicals, people who believed that Russia was headed towards an inevitable, glorious, social revolution. These were the kind of people who made up the organization – The People's Will – that would eventually assassinate the Tsar. The literature which appeared in this period of Russian history is indicative of the utopian tide sweeping Russia: upon publication in 1863, Chernyshevsky's *What is to be done?* would become a manual for young revolutionaries – most famously of course, for a young named Vladimir Ilyich Lenin. [*Awareness of historical processes*] Alexander was aware of the tide, and took steps to liberalise aspects of Russian political life: there was a relaxation of censorship between 1856 and 1867, a change that allowed Russian to read almost anything they wanted. The fact that in 1872, Marx's "Das Capital" was published in Russia, and to extraordinary success, is testament both to Nicholas' liberalism, and the wave of political radicalism after the Crimean War. The introduction of Zemstvos 1864, a form of local government assembly, was indeed designed to heavily favour local nobleman, but it was indicative of Alexander's desire to move towards a more reformed system of local government. The decentralization of power in Soviet historiography for example, has been ignored in its monumental importance: this was the first time an autocrat had sanctioned and encouraged local political activity, this was no small concession; it was a quite extraordinary piece of reform. [*Analysis and link to historiography*] Similarly, soviet historiography has attempted to exaggerate the repressive aspects of the later half of Alexander's, generally counted as being after 1866. This is however, to focus too much on the execution of radicals, and even in this there is some irony to be taken from soviet outcry that Nicholas was a repressor. Although it is true that there was an increase in some aspects of repression, the appointment of Loris-Meliokov, a politician who was dedicated to slow but steady reform towards a constitutional monarch, as minister of the interior, and Alexander's signing of the Loris-Meliokov constitution on March the 13th, the same day as his assassination point to a genuine underlying liberalism; it was not however, not liberal enough for the revolutionary tide taking hold of Russia.

Both Military and Judicial reforms **[*This does not link to the structure as alluded to in the introduction – weak*]** exemplified the unfortunate predicament of Tsar Nicholas' liberalism: although both represented the kind of extraordinary political measures unheard of before in Russia, they still failed to satisfy extreme calls for radicalization. Miliutin, the chief architect of the Military's reform, implemented a change of radical army liberalization in 1862. New recruits were better trained, and returned to their villages or towns better equipped to run their daily life and aids the general community. All draftees had access to primary education, and a real *esprit de corps* sprang up amongst the soldiers. The success of the reforms was no better demonstrated than in the 1877 Russo-Turkish war, where the soldiers worked effectively with the command structure for the first time, and a resounding victory was one. Alexander seemed to have proved that liberalizing the army could bring about military success. Yet this was not enough for many of his opponents, and in December 1879, the People's Will attempted once again to murder him. They argued that Russian needed to focus on internal liberation, and that Alexander was proving once again that the Tsarist system was one of imperialist domination. Similarly, with the Judiciary reforms, **[*Decent detail on both areas of reform*]** the implementation of some of the most progressive and fair trials in Europe was met with anger from certain sections of society: they were not sweeping enough, still prone to bias and abuse. Dominic Moon argues that although the trials were probably the greatest achievement of Alexander's regime, they happened in a climate that made it impossible for their liberal potential to be recognized. Like so many of Alexander's reforms he was liberal, just not liberal enough for radical Russia. **[*Excellent conclusion to the paragraph linking historiography with a balanced judgement*]**

In conclusion, it is of little surprise that Sophia Perovskaya, one of Alexander's assassins, would weep at her own deed. She asked herself: "Why did we do it?" The reality was that Russian revolutionaries had not seen the liberal potential of Alexander II, instead thinking of his reforms as not giving them the final results they so desired. Their desire for absolution of their original sin, for a genuinely representative government were being appeased slowly, but perhaps too slowly by Alexander who was liberalizing at autocracy's pace. [*Interesting combination of social and political history – shows depth*]Members of all radical organizations must have realised the fortune they had had only when Alexander III came into power and established a set of powerful and conservative counter-reforms. Russia had found a reformer, but he had come at the wrong time, [*Perhaps this is too speculative an assumption...*] and the Russian people were not, sadly, prepared to wait.

Chapter Three – The difference between narration and analysis

"Identifying the difference between narration and analysis was for me the most difficult, and most crucial, aspect of improving my history essays. The problem is, particularly in IB History, of attempting to separate the way you are taught with the way you write. It seemed odd to me: in class I was told stories, about men, about situations and about why nations, societies and people acted in certain ways.

"It seemed logical then when I was presented with a question, these events, stories and moments would simply be recounted. The Safe Hands approach however, encouraged me to see that there is a difference between interpretation and narration.

"Joe described the difference to me with an analogy: he said that anyone can tell you what a watch is, but that very few people can theorize or offer an explanation as to how the cogs in the watch produce the ticking of the hands. I began to think of an historical situation as a watch (bizarre as it sounds) and the social, political, military, religious, diplomatic and economic factors as the cogs which operated under the hands. This way of thinking allowed me to determine which of these cogs I thought of as more important, how they interacted, and ultimately continually link them back to the ticking of the hands.

"These principles are outlined in this chapter in the academic way in which they are ultimately to be applied. This bending of information, they weighing and checking, determining value and limitation, become for me the most enjoyable and rewarding part of writing, once I had understood the fundamental difference between the two."

One of the great difficulties students face when given feedback from their teachers is the apparently paradoxical comment: 'you need more analysis and more evidence but less narrative and be more concise.' Great. Thanks a lot. I know how frustrating this comment can be as I have made it myself on numerous occasions. What exactly does it mean, more evidence but less narrative? And what actually constitutes analysis?

The Diploma Programme History Guide Glossary of Command Terms defines 'Analyse' as: 'Break down in order to bring out the essential elements or structure.'

The language used here is interesting – 'break down' and 'bring out' suggest something almost informal, while 'essential' shows an important aspect of analysis, which is giving priority. What is, therefore, essential, and what is not? Key questions when attempting to answer any sort of question on causation. Dictionary definitions of 'analyse' fit with the IB conception. Ultimately, perhaps in simplest terms, 'analyse' means **to reveal something through careful examination**. In terms of a history essay, that means to evaluate relevant factors and reach a decision regarding the question. And that, as an explanation, is not very helpful!

This is the problem teachers have. (Ok, maybe not 'the' problem. Less money than bankers and lawyers, less respect than doctors, having to listen to every single non-teacher's opinion on Michael Gove's syllabus ideas, long holidays in which to reflect on how difficult term time can be, etc. These are also problems.)

So. The problem: it is very difficult to explain exactly what analysis is, without using many of the other command terms: evaluate, explain, discuss, contrast, compare, identify etc. It may be alphabetised, but even if it weren't, 'analyse' should be the first in the command term list. Understand what it means, and all the other terms become redundant – when you analyse properly, you cover them all.

One way to understand better what 'analyse' means is to compare it to 'narrate'. Unsurprisingly, 'narrate' is not one of the command terms. However, I would argue that it should be. Although telling the story 'as it happened' will not achieve high marks in an examination essay, it is an important part of studying History. The magnificent Ranke held that history should be written 'as it really was', which is a sort of call to narrative. (Sort of. It's all about the influence of the divine – a professor of mine demonstrated this by taking us to the Botanical Gardens to look at plants. I don't remember much about Ranke, but I do remember how romantic Botanical Gardens can be.)

Teachers will, either themselves or with readings, ensure that their students have a good sense of the chronology of events and know essentially 'what happened' before looking at how or why it did. A pertinent comparison might be with English – you cannot critically evaluate a text you haven't actually read. In the same way, a sense of 'what happened' is essential to History. And here lies the problem outlined in the introduction: there is so much narrative material to cover that teachers are not always able to focus on the skills needed to analyse it. The Safe Hands approach creates an analytical framework through its structure and execution and forces you to avoid writing essays overly reliant on narrative.

Let's think about what the examiners are looking for in terms of analysis and narrative. The events or 'facts' within a topic are covered in the mark schemes with the following phrases: 'Historical context', 'Historical processes', 'Historical knowledge', and 'evidence base'. In later chapters we will look more carefully at how to use and integrate evidence and historiography, but for now let's consider this in terms of analysis and narrative.

Essentially, demonstrating awareness of 'Historical context' and 'Historical processes' is to show an understanding of the broad narrative arc of a topic. History as a subject is not a story, but there is a story or narrative at the heart of History. Consider the Russia topic we have been looking at. The period from Alexander II to Lenin's death is a tale of incredible change marked by hugely dramatic events: massive social reform, autocracy, nationalism and liberalism, the Great War, the revolutions of 1917, the Civil War and the establishment of one of the major political states and ideologies that helped to define the Twentieth Century. It's quite a yarn and there are countless novels written about the period, either contemporary or historical. The story involves ambition, justice, violence, and even sex. No surprise that it is such a fertile ground for novelists. Remember: the narrative arc of History is reflected in fiction and cinema, not the other way around. The story, in terms of a basic conception of 'what happened', is everything.

But what then of Historical processes and context? Well, 'the study of History is a study of causes', as E.H. Carr states in 'What is History'. A further insight is to think about the classic causation dichotomy: that History is more significantly affected by Great Men or longer term socio-economic forces. Carr attaches to the former the 'Cleopatra's Nose' theory of History – essentially that history is chance, a series of accidents of specific, human decision-making potentially based upon irrational feelings. This idea holds that it is the great men – Hitler, Stalin, Napoleon, Luther etc – that make History; they bend society to their will and impose their own structures and we deal with the consequences.

The second idea does not discount the impact of the Great Men, but seeks to explain their existence or possibility, if you like, through a careful, long-term examination of socio-economic forces. This can have an interesting moral impact. When studying the Holocaust, for example, it feels ethically preferable to blame one man's twisted vision of humanity rather than to attempt to trace its roots or attribute culpability to society in general. The Intentionalist/Structuralist debate covers this and we won't go into it here. But it does demonstrate that these two very broad theories of History are not in any way exclusive.

I have simplified these ideas to try to make one point about processes and context: at IB level you need to show awareness that both individuals and societal currents are essential to narrative understanding. And this is what Historical processes and context are all about: the impact and consequences of individual decisions interacting with societal trends. 'Processes', perhaps, can be understood as specific events or policies and their results, and 'context' as broader aspects of society – political, social and economic.

The point is that, while a basic interpretation, this conceptual division will help you to ensure that you hit both parts of the mark scheme and consider both context and processes in your essays.

So narrative is intimately connected to a successful essay, but how to show understanding of it without simply telling the story?

Here we need to assess the terms 'historical knowledge' and 'evidence base'. Regarding the exam, these terms involve the syllabus – the bullet pointed lists, which show the content you are supposed to have covered during the course. Although these lists are not exhaustive, they do offer a fairly thorough picture of 'what you need to know'.

Now, an examiner is very likely – but not certain – to know your essay topic very well. He does not need to be told what happened. Again, there is a pertinent comparison to be made with English: you are not expected to write about the plot of a novel or to explain how the story might unfold in the unseen text – you are looking at the impact of the text, and how that was created. In History, essays that are dominated by narrative may well show some understanding of processes and context, *but only in terms of the narrative arc*. An effective essay must use the 'evidence base' and 'historical knowledge' to support analysis and not supplant it.

Analysis, put simply, is an examination of the 'how' and 'why', and not an exposition of the 'what' (the content or narrative).

Let's have a look at an example question:

'The Duma system was purely a means of maintaining power.' Discuss this statement with reference to Nicholas II up to 1914.

In terms of content, this question involves the second and third of the bullet points above. Broadly speaking, the question is looking at opposition to Nicholas II and his attempt to appease and yet secure his position as Tsar. Some of the key events and names are mentioned in the syllabus – the Russo-Japanese War, 1905 Revolution, Stolypin, etc – and these give a clear indication as to some of the evidence that needs to be assessed. But there is also another type of Historical knowledge, which I like to call 'anecdotal evidence'. This type of evidence (which we will look at in more depth in a later chapter) can add colour to an essay and show an impressive depth of understanding and knowledge. It is the kind of story or detail that may highlight the absurdity of a particular situation or event. Anecdotal evidence does not mean telling an anecdote, but using a detail to enhance your essay. If nothing else, a colourful detail or two will improve the examiner's experience of reading your work. Just don't let them dominate! Writing essays – and though this guide may be a case against this, I've always said to my students to do as I say not as I do – is not about making your audience chuckle at how drily witty you are.

Let's now look at an example from a paragraph from an essay answering the question above to show the relationship between narrative and analysis and how to effectively strike a balance. Using the thematic structure explained in chapter two, the student here has divided his essay into social concessions, political changes, and economic reforms. This section is taken from the paragraph on political changes.

In terms of the maintenance of his own political power, the Duma was undoubtedly the greatest potential challenge to the Tsar's political authority; an organization he saw both as radical and fundamentally anti-Tsarist. The welcome that the Duma delegates received in the Winter Palace's Coronation hall in their first convocation, exemplified the way that the Tsar saw the Duma: the delivered a curt speech, addressed his supporters and ignored his Duma enemies, promised to uphold Tsardom, and promptly left. The Duma he reasoned, was not going to limit his power: he may have signed the October manifesto, but the 87th article allowed him to pass laws in "time of emergency" without the Duma's approval, and he was still convinced that his power had been handed down to him from God, something that however democratic the Duma was, it could not match. The Duma ministers themselves had visions of bringing about radical change, but this was not going to be tolerated by the Tsar. In their first congregation in 1906, the Duma aggressively demanded an amnesty for political prisoners in the Peter & Paul St. Petersburg jail. The Tsar ignored their demands, asking instead for the Duma's approval on a new laundry service and a greenhouse at the University of Dorpat. The Tsar had congregated many political enemies in the Duma, yet he had absolute power over them, could monitor their actions, and at the same time regularly humiliate them. Far from being an instrument to maintain power, the Duma was largely ignored.

This extract neatly captures the essence of the Duma and Nicholas' intention for it. The student shows that while the Tsar felt he had to make concessions to the political opposition and felt the move to be opposed to the autocratic tradition of the Tsarist system, equally, he did not take the democratic organ seriously. The first sentence of the paragraph captures this thesis and introduces us to the student's argument. The paragraph then unfolds with evidence in support of this. We do not learn the story of the Duma, but we are given details as to Nicholas' reaction to it both from an anecdotal and political policy perspective. The mention of the welcome the Duma delegates receives illustrates Nicholas' offhand manner when dealing with them. The details of the 87th article and the emergency laws reveals that, despite the appearance of democracy, power ultimately remained in the hands of the Tsar. The far-reaching political and social ambitions of the Duma delegates is also alluded to, and the Tsar's response is both faintly humorous and very revealing – he saw the Duma as a means to passing mandates on laundry and gardening services.

This combination of specific detail with colourful stories acts as both narrative and analysis. Using the evidence, the thesis statement is supported and developed; we are not given a chronological outline of the process to the formation of the Duma, but rather an insight into how it worked and how Nicholas believed he could use its platform to appease and yet reinforce his power. The evidence is placed within the structural context of the Safe Hands approach, is bookended by thesis statements and links back to the introduction. Therefore, there is little danger of too much narrative and an analytical approach is ensured. Here is an example of 'revealing through examination' (my basic definition of analysis at the beginning of the chapter). The student has looked carefully at key aspects of the Duma and drawn his conclusions as to Nicholas' intentions, in terms of the question. It is clear that the student believes that the Duma was a means of maintaining power, but that he also understands the implications of the question, i.e. that concessions and appeasement were a part of this process.

Regarding the mark scheme, this approach hits these key requirements in the upper bands:

In-depth and accurate historical knowledge is applied consistently and convincingly to support critical commentary. In addition answers may reveal a high level of conceptual ability.

Assessment Objective 3: Synthesis and Evaluation

- *Develop critical commentary using the evidence base*
- *Synthesise by integrating evidence and critical commentary*

Let's now look at the full essay.

'The Duma system was purely a means of maintaining power.' Discuss this statement with reference to Nicholas II up to 1914.

To argue that the duma system was a means of maintaining power in Russia is to assume that it was actively involved in important state affairs. It would be a fallacy to think that, after November 1907, the date of the calling of the Third Duma, it wielded any political power, or that the Tsar and Stolypin actively used to it to "maintain power". [*Balanced thesis that considers both arguments*] The role of the Duma in the maintenance of power can thus be divided into three broad areas: social concessions, political changes, and economic reforms. [*Thematic structure, plus a level of detail*]

59

The Duma was a major political concession on the Tsar's part as a way of maintaining social order and ensuring that a powerful social revolution did not sweep him from power. [*Shows Tsarist intent plus makes connection between political policy and social impact*] The Duma was not a compromise, a hand of peace towards a populace that in 1905 had rebelled against oppressive Tsarist measures, but a way of creating the semblance [*Subtle use of language to show intent*] of representative popular power in the government's sphere of influence. This was key in ensuring a slowing down in the popular opposition. Nicholas' acceptance of the October manifesto's demands for greater popular representation on 17th of October 1905 was signed with a heavy heart, [*Perhaps a historian's view would add authority here*] and little intention of genuine change. The Duma was effective in helping him maintaining power, as it allowed him to introduce socially repressive measures at a time where he seemed to be liberalizing. This meant that the Tsar could attack the political bite of the socialist uprising on The 15th of December; hundreds of members of the Petrograd Soviet and other smaller independent soviets were arrested. With the revolutionary sentiment quelled by his acceptance of the Duma, and its more radical representatives quickly jailed, Nicholas took advantage of the conservative tide (perhaps the only tide left after the first Duma's calling) to re-establish himself as a strong political leader by the beginning of 1906. To argue that after this time however, the Duma played a significant role in social Russian affairs is to grossly overestimate its power. The Tsar had used the Duma for its primary social purpose in the months following the revolution, after that, it had little social influence of any use to him. [*Neat summary of the paragraph, which links to the introduction/thesis*]

In terms of the maintenance of his own political power, the Duma was undoubtedly the greatest potential challenge to the Tsar's political authority; an organization he saw both as radical and fundamentally anti-Tsarist. [*Sets up thesis and introduces analytical use of evidence, NOT narration*] The welcome that the Duma delegates received in the Winter Palace's Coronation hall in their first convocation, exemplified the way that the Tsar saw the Duma: the delivered a short curt speech, addressed his supports and ignored his Duma enemies, promised to uphold Tsardom, and promptly left. The Duma he reasoned, was not going to limit his power: he may have signed the October manifesto, but the 87th article allowed him to pass laws in "time of emergency" without the Duma's approval, and he was still convinced that his power had been handed down to him from God, something that however democratic the Duma was, it could not match. The Duma ministers themselves had visions of bringing about radical change, but this was not going to be tolerated by the Tsar. In their first congregation in 1916, the Duma aggressively demanded an amnesty for political prisoner's in the Peter & Paul St. Petersburg jail. The Tsar ignored their demands, asking instead for the Duma's approval on a new laundry service and a greenhouse at the University of Dorpat. The Tsar had congregated many political enemies in the Duma, yet he had absolute power over them, could monitor their actions, and at the same time regularly humiliate them. Far from being an instrument to maintain power, the Duma was largely ignored. It could do nothing for example, when Stolypin, decided in 1906 to execute or exile without trial some 60,000 political detainees, as well as closing down hundreds of revolutionary newspapers. [*Effective use of evidence*] Stolypin, his great hero being Bismarck, saw the Duma along more Prussian than British lines. It was in his eyes and instrument of the state, an extra layer of bureaucracy used to enact policies into law. His dissolving of Duma after Duma, until finally a third filled with, as he put it, "responsible" and "statesmanlike" people, emphasizing his own indifference to the apparent political concessions that underpinned the Duma. Although successful in the short-term in helping to re-establish Tsarist political power, it corrupted the open willing and liberal middle class Russian's had hoped for political reform. [*Shows awareness/understanding of historical processes*] It was these men, men like Prince Lvov, the eventual leader of the provisional government, who would support the revolution in February 1917. Therefore, although successful in the short term in maintaining power, the long-term effect of the Duma was bad for Tsarist rule.

The economic reforms that Stolypin desired to put in place emphasized the way that the Duma had become impotent and had long ceased to be a means of maintaining power. [*Thematic link to thesis*] Stolypin wanted to move away from backward peasant practices and introduce a new modernizing sweep of agricultural and economic reforms, which he hoped would help create a new Russian peasant middle class, invested in Tsarist rule. He realized that although he thought of the Duma as perfunctory semblance of democracy, they were capable of slowing down his land reforms. The second Duma, which was formed in July of 1906 with him as Prime Minister, still had many members who, coming from peasant and landowning backgrounds and feeling as if Tsarism had already broken too many promises, refused to support Stolypin's bid for property. One peasant deputy, from Stolypin's own Saratov province embodied the frustration, both historic and current of the peasant class, when he confront conservative delegates in the Duma by saying: "We know about your property, for we were your property once. My uncle was exchanged for a greyhound". [*Lovely use of anecdotal evidence to demonstrate thesis*] Stolypin did however acknowledge the legitimizing effect that Duma agreement to his policies would have, giving them a semblance of popular weight. To ensure victory and support then, he dissolved the second Duma, heavily influencing the elections to ensure that he had the majority of the support, and his reform bills were promptly passed. It's no surprise that the third Duma would stay in power for five years and pass 200 pieces of legislation on some 2500 bills. Stolypin proved that the Duma was purely a means of maintaining power: he needed it to pass the reforms that he hoped would bring Russia a middle class peasant class. However, he also realized that the Duma was just that, a means could be manipulated to suit his will. After 1907, by the time of the fourth and fifth Dumas, the Duma had become purely a legal means of retaining power, not an active maintenance body. [*Shows understanding of the historical context and places the evidence squarely within this to support the thesis*]

In conclusion, to look at the use of the Duma system between 1905 and 1914 as period of continuous maintenance would be a fallacy. Instead it should be noted that between 1905 and 1907, the Duma was important in helping to quell popular anger towards Nicholas, legitimize reforms and help to provide political weight to the repression of hundreds of revolutionaries. However, after 1907, and the calling of the third Duma, the Duma was not actively involved in the maintenance of power. This was, in essence, because it had no power. Instead, it became a legal organization, complementing the political work of Stolypin and the Tsar with a democratic facade. [*Supports and reestablishes thesis*] However, it was to be the Duma's leaders, disregarded and discarded by the Tsar, who would go on to be integral parts of the February uprising, and eventually play a key role in the formation of the provisional government.

Chapter four – The use of evidence

"Once I began to understand the difference between analysis and narrative in an essay, choosing different sources of evidence and finding a balance between them came to be at the centre of my essays. I had a tendency to rely too much on anecdotal evidence, and the Safe Hands approach encouraged me to reduce my dependence on it: ultimately, it is important to realize that anecdotal evidence, in excess, doesn't carry the same weight as factual and statistical evidence. Nonetheless, this is when the writing gets really fun.

"Finding meaty statistical and factual evidence and combining it with vivid, colourful and attractive anecdotal and historical view is genuinely enjoyable. If the structure and introduction provide the frame and skeleton for the essay to function, and the analysis gives the essay its flesh, then choice of evidence is the way in which you choose to dress the essay, giving it a sense of character.

"This is perhaps where the liberty provided by the safe hands structure becomes obvious: being secure in the way the essay will unfold allows you to really enjoy fleshing it out."

In mark scheme terms, an effective evidence-based essay comes down to these two bullet points:

- *Develop critical commentary using the evidence base*
- *Synthesise by integrating evidence and critical commentary*

It is clear that evidence alone is not sufficient for the upper mark bands and that the skill required for a successful essay is the integration of evidence within the analysis, or critical commentary. The Safe Hands structure enables this integration, as hinted at in previous chapters. With each section linked to the thesis, as outlined in the introduction, by a topic sentence, paragraphs are built from the argument up – examples are dripped into the paragraph alongside commentary to support the ideas proposed in the initial topic sentence. To do this successfully the balance detailed in Chapter Three must be applied. Be sure that your use of evidence is done so as a series of supporting examples and doesn't take the form of a narrative or story.

Before we look at the techniques used to do this, let's consider what actually constitutes evidence. We can refer again to E.H. Carr's 'What is History?' here and specifically to his discussion of what makes a 'fact', 'historical'. His point boils down to, essentially, the canon. If historians agree that a fact is worthy of being considered 'historical', then it is. I suppose this means that it is written down and referred to and attributed. In other words, when I teach a group of students it is undeniably happening, is a fact. We are all there and witnesses to it. However, this is not a 'historical fact' in the same way that, say, we know about Hitler's failure as an artist as a young man. Perhaps, if one of my students were to go on to an especially noteworthy career, and he or she were to explain the influence of their History teacher and even pick out a particular lesson in which he had a profound impact on them, then I suppose the 'event' might one day be considered a historical fact and used as evidence in some way. Not to denigrate my students – or myself – but I'm not sure this is very likely.

What is the difference between a fact and an event? Or a chain of events? Or a series of consequences? And can we ever really distinguish between different types of fact? To what extent is a fact ever actually indisputable? These are questions we need not concern ourselves with too much here, but it is worth considering the different types of evidence that you have as IB students at your disposal. The reason: the *arrangement* of your evidence is what is crucial. Professional Historians do not ascertain the facts as much as present them to us. That's your job too. And to do it properly, you need to know what kind of things you have at your disposal.

I have identified five basic types of evidence, all of which are acceptable for your use, all of which you will have come across in text books and articles and lessons, and all of which can be broadly described as 'facts'. Points 3-5 could also be termed as 'sources'.

1. Dates
2. Statistics
3. Anecdotes
4. Doctrine
5. Historians' views (in terms of quotations or statements as distinct from historiography, which we will look at in depth in the following chapter)

Dates and **statistics** are, on the surface, fairly straightforward. They are figures or numbers and generally 'neutral', in the sense that even if the figure or number does not necessarily reflect reality (see the fudging of industrial production output figures in Stalin's Russia) the number itself remains as a record and therefore 'fact'. We can dispute statistics, of course, and they can be used to make different arguments, but they exist as they are as pieces of evidence.

Anecdotes are slightly more complicated. I made reference to anecdotal evidence in the previous chapter as a means of adding colourful details to your essays. A darkly humorous or emotionally moving anecdote will bring your essay to life and the examiner will – as long as the story is used as an example and doesn't dominate the essay – appreciate it. I'm talking about the kind of thing you'll find in books like Richard Grunberger's 'A Social History of the Third Reich'. In this superb text, Grunberger addresses all aspects of Nazi society – children, women, film, art, radio, television etc. – and without ever undermining the serious tone and nature of the work, includes anecdotal evidence of absurd Nazi behaviour, particularly regarding their attitudes towards women and culture.

There is, I felt when I first read the book as a sixth-former, something reassuring about discovering that leading Nazis (on top of their despicable, inhumane actions and opinions) were sexist, boorish and lacking in any cultural discernment or sophistication. The story of a high-ranking Nazi, for example, who kept a naked portrait of his wife on his wall and proudly unveiled it and the end of his dinner parties has stayed with me. Perhaps because he was so proud of his wife's charms that the portrait was eventually not considered a good enough likeness and he would parade her around the table allowing his guests to revel in her Teutonic nakedness. This is an awful, blackly comic story, but a revealing one too. Think about how it connects to the sinister aspects of the Nazi ideal of Kinder, Küche, Kirche. Equally, think about how it portrays this ranking Nazi in terms of his unenlightened vulgarity and how that might represent the party as a whole.

However, how effective would it be in an examination essay? The anecdote may fit into a response on Nazi domestic or social policies, but it is fairly long and the analytical point that it reveals is very broad on the one hand – basically, that the Nazi party was run by sexist idiots – but also specific in terms of the role of women in the Third Reich. It's a great story for class, but I'm not sure it would work in a 45/50-minute exam situation.

Better are the anecdotes used in the last chapter regarding Nicholas' welcome of the Duma delegates and his request for laundry facilities. Here, these 'facts' support the student's broader thesis and are connected directly to it. The best anecdotal evidence will do this – a snippet of social history that illuminates your argument but does not distract from it. Yes, the examiner wants to enjoy reading your essays, but he doesn't want to see someone showing off his 'obscure' knowledge. This is not the same as 'depth'. In the essay at the end of this chapter, I will identify further examples of effective anecdotal evidence.

By **Doctrine** I mean the political ideas of key historical figures as published in their pamphlets, memoirs or tracts. Most obviously, I'd identify examples such as 'Mein Kampf', Lenin's 'What is to be done?' or 'The Communist Manifesto'. These works offer terrific insight into the mindset and ideals of these political figures and raise interesting questions about motivation and intention. As evidence, they can be used to demonstrate long-term political or ideological ambition and can be drawn into comparisons even with policy. Think

about Lenin's adaptation of Marxist doctrine and his sloganeering –
Peace, Bread and Land – as well as his claims to be the 'vanguard of
the Proletariat', and his fluctuating economic ideology – War
Communism and then the N.E.P. It's an interesting argument to
consider his flexibility and to what extent his aims were dictated
ultimately by a desire for power as opposed to a staunch,
unwavering belief in his ideals, which can appear to be the way he
mythologized his role in the growth of the Bolshevik party and
October Revolution.

The question of intention is worth addressing briefly. Collingwood
wrote that 'all history is the history of thought'. While of course all
sources such as memoirs or diaries or political manifestos are
philosophically 'impure' (in the sense that even in our private
writings we are conscious of portraying ourselves in a certain light
and perhaps unable to write the unadorned truth) these doctrinal
pieces of evidence offer a sense of the thinking behind the policies
that we are unable to glean from elsewhere. Like anecdotal evidence,
a concise, well-chosen reference to a piece of writing can be used to
effectively support a thesis (for example that the N.E.P was an
expedient decision and demonstrated that Lenin was not as steadfast

in his beliefs as his writings may suggest) and also to add more of that colour I mentioned in the last chapter.

Finally, **Historians' views**. I mentioned that I intend this to be distinct from Historiography, which we will consider carefully in the next chapter. In this case, I mean a short, revealing quotation, which, while providing an insight related to the question, will also give your essay weight and demonstrate the depth of your reading and knowledge. On a very simplistic level, consider this quotation from the essay we will look at later in the chapter in response to a question on the revolutions of 1917: 'As Orlando Figes puts it in his seminal work "A People's Tragedy" – "It all began with bread"'. This quotation demonstrates that the student understands the economic and social issues that helped to cause the February revolution, and distils this into a very well chosen comment from one of the preeminent historians of the period. Furthermore, look at the drama and simplicity of the phrase: more colour and style. This is the kind of quotation that can be very effective as evidence – concise and punchy and adding authority. 'Bread' represents the social and economic problems of Russia in 1917, and the student captures this sense brilliantly by using this quotation.

So those are the different 'types' of evidence you might use, and now the question is how you use it. The key word is integration: you need to combine critical commentary with supporting evidence. As I mentioned earlier, the Safe Hands approach structure creates an excellent basis for this, but there is more to it than simply following this structure.

Remember my basic definition of analysis? To reveal through examination. An effective way to think about how to use evidence is this: **to reveal through example**. Try to think of your use of evidence as analysis itself. Ask yourself the following question: what does this example reveal? If it tells us something that is related to the question, then simply selecting it is a process of analysis. Deciding which facts you will use to develop and support your arguments is an analytical process. The important thing is to make it clear in your employment of evidence that it is a demonstration of a point and not a narrative. One way to do this is to sandwich the evidence with explanation. This will – at the very least – be the thesis statement at the top of the paragraph, and a concluding sentence, which will bring it back to the overall structure.

Analysis is the revealing of something through examination. Evidence is the thing that shows this reveal to be demonstrable. Think about the essay in the last chapter. The thesis suggests the Tsar did not take the Duma seriously, that he sanctioned it out of appearances. The student revealed this idea through his research. And what piece of evidence supports this reveal? The welcoming speech. It supports the thesis and tells us something about the Tsar. It supports the reveal, but also reveals something itself.

Let's have a look at part of a paragraph from an essay answering the question: **Compare and contrast the nature of the two revolutions of 1917**.

This sense of an emboldened Duma, combined with the growing feelings of political embitterment towards the government, created the political conditions in February of 1917 for the revolution. There was no single figure of paramount importance. On the 23rd of February 1917, orator after orator clambered up onto a huge statue of Tsar

Alexander III in Znamenskaya square, delivering revolutionary speeches to the crowd (some 100,000 men and women), capturing the very essence of the uprising. Of course there were more or less politicised members of the public and the workers, but the revolution was in essence, popular.

The student's thesis in this paragraph on the political aspects of the question is, put simply, to show the difference between the popular nature of the February revolution in contrast to the Bolshevik Coup D'état in October. There is a development of this thesis in the first sentence. We learn of 'an emboldened Duma' and 'growing feelings of political embitterment', which demonstrates that anti-Tsarist sentiment is both felt by official political opposition, but also on the streets. The popular aspect of the uprising is then enhanced and supported in the next sentence: the thesis is developed – 'There was no single figure of paramount importance' – and then evidence is employed to support this. We have a date, and a concise anecdote, a piece of social history that demonstrates the reality of February 1917. The final sentence in the example concedes that of course there were degrees of political involvement – offering balance – but also emphasizes the student's thesis, that February was popular 'in essence'.

Look at the way each sentence builds on the preceding sentence: the first is a development of the topic sentence at the beginning of the paragraph (which you will see at the end of the chapter); the second takes the thesis a step further; the third provides support for the thesis with a date and a story; and the final sentence re-establishes the thesis in the context of this example.

This snippet is only part of a longer paragraph, but it offers a formula – for each point you wish to make, you should be able to do it in three or four sentences: a development of your thesis acting as the analytical reveal; an example that demonstrates this; and a final contextualizing point – how it all fits into the paragraph thesis (political, social or economic) and the overall essay thesis (as established in the introduction).

Let's now look at the whole essay.

Compare and contrast the nature of the two revolutions in 1917

It would be convenient to argue that in many ways the October 1917 revolution was an extension of February: after all, it was the same cocktail of social, economic and political problems which plagued Russia's respective rulers. *[Demonstrates understanding of the implications of the question]* However, that would be to ignore the ideological manipulation by the Bolshevik party, the role of key individuals, primarily Lenin, and the scale of Russian disillusionment with the Dual Power system in Petrograd. *[Identifies key content and develops thesis]* Thus there are three key, broad, areas of difference and comparison: *political changes, social problems*, and *economic complaints*. *[Thematic structure, plus detail]*

Looking at the political nature of the two revolutions exposes the difference in their scale and motivation. *[Links to introduction]* The February revolution was in large part a popular uprising, stemming in a political sense from a long building antagonism towards Tsar Nicholas II. The Duma system instated in 1905 was coming to be thought by the Russian people as an instrument of oppression rather than a democratic voice for the people. As this view became increasingly apparent, its members, namely future head of the Provisional Government Prince Lvov, argued that it was time to "turn away from the ghosts" and support openly a democratic revolution. This sense of an emboldened Duma, combined with the growing feelings of political embitterment towards the government, created the political conditions in February of 1917 for the revolution. There was no single figure of paramount importance; on the 23rd of February 1917, orator after orator clambered up onto a huge statue of Tsar Alexander III in Znamenskaya square, delivering revolutionary speeches to the crowd (some 100,000 men and women), capturing the very essence of the uprising: of course there were more or less politicised members of the public and the workers, but the revolution was in essence, popular. *[Paragraph contains great variety of types of evidence]*

In October however, it was the political will of one man, Lenin, which dictated the outcome of the revolution. *[Note: comparative structure within the themes – there is a thematic structure, but within each thematic section, one paragraph covers February and another October. This sets up an excellent form of analysis and comparison]* Propelled by the widely held belief within Russia, and even the Dual power, that "Counter-revolution was inevitable", Lenin and the Bolshevik party took control by attacking a weak government that had struggled to deal with economic problems and become increasingly unpopular over its unwillingness to withdraw from the war. Lenin placed himself at the centre of the "protection of the revolution" and appealed to old and simplistic political arguments about oppression that stemmed from 1914. He aligned his own political ideology to that of deluded Russian soldiers and sailors to create a revolutionary group capable of capturing power. It was no surprise then that when the "storming" of the Winter Palace did happen, that there were probably no more than 10,000 people involved: October was a coup d'état carried out by Lenin and the Bolshevik party, not a popular uprising.

The greatest social problem that faced both Tsar Nicholas II and The Dual power system was undoubtedly the war, *[Links war to the domestic social situation, thus connecting theme and content]* which brought about revolution in the first because of mass popular unrest, and in the second because of the politicization of heavily armed officer class.

After a briefly uplifting moment on the 4th of June 1915, and the Brusilov offensive, Russian morale in their army had been destroyed thanks to incompetent handling by Tsar Nicholas' government. In 1916, as the "Great Retreat" gathered momentum, vicious anti-German rumours about the Tsarina and her court began to circulate. As with any major ideological shift, it was not the truth or untruth of these rumours, rather the effect they had in radicalizing the populous and turning the public against the Tsarist dynasty. The old perception of the Tsar as the god appointed representative for the Russian people was fast eroding: as this perception changed, there was space for a radical ideological shift, which meant that the social feeling against the Tsar emboldened people to go out onto the streets, begin riots, go on strikes and release anti-Tsarist propaganda openly. In this sense, the social nature of the February 1917 revolution was a liberating one: an angry populace discarded old idealizations of the Tsarist regime, and instead opted for a popular, revolutionary uprising. *[Captures the essence of the February uprising in terms of the student's thesis – connecting to the introduction]*

The War also dominated as the greatest social problem for the provisional government. *[Continues thematic comparison between February and October]* The Allied rejection of the "Stockholm Peace Conference" proved that the failings of the old tsarist regime made the provisional governments position even more difficult. The war's unpopularity was compounded by Kerensky's later journeys to the front, where impassioned speeches had begun to wear thin on soldiers staving and freezing to death. *[Excellent anecdotal evidence]* This created the conditions for the politicization of an officer and sailor class that had the military means to run and start a powerful uprising. It is no surprise that the Kronstadt sailors plays such a large part in the July days *[Showing understanding of connections/context/historical processes]* and that a large military and sailor presence was part of the storming of the winter palace. Lenin appealed to simple military desires

79

with "All Power to the Soviet!" This allowed him to harness the support of people like the Kronstadt soldiers, who were vital in providing the military support that the coup d'état needed, and at the same time the ideology was vague enough to garner mild popular support. The combination of these two social changes, the radicalization of the officers and the disappointment with the provisional government paved the way for Lenin's seizure of power in October 1917. *[Excellent concluding line, bringing the key elements together]*

Economic problems in Russia provided the final spark for the beginning of the Februrary1917 revolution, and 8 months later would add to disillusionment with the provisional government that placed Lenin in a strategic position of power. As Orlando Figes puts it in his seminal work *A People's Tragedy* "It all began with bread". *[Excellent synthesis of the economic situation – equally, could be used in the Social section]* The bread shortages caused by a bitter Russian winter meant that looting, violence in the streets and starvation had begun to take hold in Petrograd. This opened the way for a swath of revolutionary sentiment: the promise of the city's radicals to feed the masses, and their blaming of the Russian economic problems on "Germans" and "Jews" appealed to broad xenophobic sentiments that pervaded Russia during the First World War. *[Good link with patriotic start to the war – historical processes]* The instigation of these accusations further increased revolutionary sentiment, and the economic spark began the first public demonstration that would eventually break out into full-scale revolution

Economic problems for the provisional government created conditions by which its own members refused to accept economic reality, and their own inability to deal with the

Russia's economic condition, and aided a Bolshevik seizure of power. *[Shows conceptual thinking – Bolsheviks offered solutions that were essentially impractical for the PG]* The ascension to power of the provisional government may have been on a tide of collective revolutionary sentiment, but that same tide could not sweep away Russia's underlying economic problems. The rise of inflation throughout 1917 served only to increase the deflation that the Russian people felt after February: one of the great revolutionary hopes, the return of bread, had been a great failure. Lenin manipulated this with his slogan "Peace, Bread & Land", harnessing the economic delusion of people, garnering support for the Bolsheviks under a broad banner, with many supporters of "Peace Bread & Land" knowing little of the party's other intentions. *[Develops the point made above and adds evidence]* This broad support however, helped Lenin and the Bolsheviks to establish themselves as the greatest opposition to the provisional government, and when the time came in October 1917, carry out a coup d'état without the opposition of many of the Petrograd's people, who hoped that finally that economic revolutionary promise would be fulfilled.

In conclusion, it seems that political, social and economic factors combined in both the February and October revolutions to create the conditions for the both. It was the failure of the Tsarist political systems and the Dumas which allowed which provoked the rise of radicalism. For Lenin it was his political manipulation of the provisional government and a broad appeal to the idea of the "counter-revolution" which helped gain the political support needed for the revolution. Socially and politically, the war and an ailing economy destroyed both Nicholas' II and the Provisional Government's hopes for stability; the war deeply unpopular, proved to be the end of Tsarist adulation, ironically, in October of 1917, war and economic failures would also prove the end of the adulation of the idealized form of revolution, both of which allowed revolutionary forces to take

81

hold. However, one fundamental difference lies at the heart of the two revolutions: February 1917 was a mass uprising, orchestrated, run in a disorganized fashion by the Russian people; October 1917 however, was an organized military coup d'état organized by Vladimir Ilyich Lenin. *[Essence of the thesis. However, this conclusion is a little long for an exam situation]*

Chapter five – The importance of Historiography

"When I first encountered historiography, at the beginning of my IB Higher Level History Course, I thought of it as a sort of trick: a way of demonstrating that you were a more 'advanced' student, and a side-corridor into a 7.

"I was not only mistaken, but limited in my appreciation of what historiography was.

"Only when I began reading extensive books on particular historical periods – particularly Orland Figes' A People's Tragedy – did I begin to realize that historiography is an extended form of what it is that we do when writing essays.

"I would recommend, to anyone who is finding history dull, to begin reading celebrated historians and historical works. They are full of the analysis, supported by extraordinary extensive, funny, moving and interesting evidence. Once you begin to appreciate what they do, you can attempt to imitate their style, thinking and analytical approach to writing. Similarly, you begin to doubt, question and disagree with aspects of what you read. This evaluation of historiography is perhaps the most personally engaging and academically rigorous way to use historiography in essays. And all captured in the Safe Hands structure.

"Finally, I think historiography displays the humanity of history: there is perhaps a tendency in textbooks to de-personalize history. Situations begin to take a sense that feels somehow detached from the people who participated in them. For the first time I began to feel a bridge between English literature, sociology, anthropology and history.

This was not only exhilarating but rewarding, but perhaps most importantly, fun."

When you first start an undergraduate History degree, it can feel that all history is essentially historiography. You are given readings and asked to consider different interpretations and ideas and try to contextualize them within your own understanding of a topic or period. At IB level, there is a certain amount of this too. Your teacher will likely give you an overview of the key opinions on the topics you are studying and show you how these have changed over time. Additionally, you will look at textbooks to provide the basic narrative and interpretations. Many of these textbooks have excellent summaries of the historiography and suggestions for further reading on the periods on which they focus. (I am thinking principally of the terrific Heinemann Advanced History Series, and specifically of the books written by Jonathan Bromley on Russia and Philip Pedley on Germany, both of who taught me when I was at school.)

As a History student, one of the first things you'll come to understand is that you are extremely unlikely to come up with an original theory or interpretation. This should not be discouraging.

The skills you will learn are about processing huge amounts of information – both content and interpretation – and making decisions based on this assimilation in terms of priority: you learn to place ideas and events in context in order to articulate your arguments and opinions. In this aspect, historiography is vital.

History is an active subject: ideas change and grow and reading around a subject and keeping abreast of current theory is important both for the student and teacher. A teacher that doesn't read History for pleasure or research is unlikely to provide the dynamism you need at IB level. Communicating a sense of History as an exciting, organic subject is an important means to engaging students and dispelling the myth that History is a dead subject about dead people. The historians dictate the subject; *that* is History. The content is merely what happened and cannot change. 'Even God cannot change the past,' as Agathon is reputed to have said. Historians, though, can change the way we *view* the past, and that is a hugely exhilarating element of the subject. Furthermore, if we agree that history is an active subject and that theories and ideas will develop through argument and counter-argument, then showing understanding of this (and the reasons for it) reveals you are committed student who has considerable depth of knowledge and passion.

Why else then is it important? A starting point is a practical one: the mark scheme. Let's have a look at the historiography related points in the upper mark band for Paper Three.

There may be evaluation of different approaches to, and interpretations of, historical issues and events. This evaluation is integrated effectively into the answer to support and supplement the argument. *In addition, an awareness of the reasons for circumstances that produced differing and often conflicting historical interpretations is present.*

Assessment objective 3: Synthesis and evaluation

• **Evaluate different approaches to, and interpretations of, historical issues and events**

There's a slight oddity about the first point above. This comes from the highest band in the mark scheme, yet the second word 'may' suggests that it is not necessary to achieve marks in this band. However, in this band, all of the basic points are supplemented with a line or two in italics. Here, the requirement is to show awareness and understanding of why there are differing views. The way in which it is phrased suggests that this element is required to achieve the very highest marks, which, by implication, suggests that the first point is too. Why then 'may'? Is it up to an examiner to judge what is really necessary or not? And what guidance can a teacher give when faced with this apparent ambiguity?

These three questions can be answered like this: Don't know (though maybe as it follows on from the lower band and they forgot to change it); ultimately, yes, though they work within guidelines and there is moderation; a teacher needs to give his students the advice which is least likely to backfire – in this case, it means include historiography and try to show why there are different interpretations. In other words: cover everything. This, sadly, takes us back to the problems outlined in the introduction about the size and weight of syllabus and mark scheme requirements.

This is a minor gripe, but one which does reflect something of the problems of Higher Level History. Let's, as we have been throughout this guide, think about practicalities and how the Safe Hands approach can help produce an essay with an effective level of historiographical depth.

The principal, non-italicized mark scheme requirement can be broken down into two parts:

1) You need to know some historians' views/interpretations

2) You need to integrate these into your answers

To achieve the first, you need to have either (and preferably both) covered a range of interpretations in class or read up around the topics on your own. The second is much like the use of evidence: use the historiography to support your argument or provide balance with a counter-argument. The difference is that, while your essays will contain a large amount of evidence, you will need to use the historiography more sparingly as an essay that reads like a survey of historians' opinions will not be a successful one.

Here the Safe Hands structure works very well. Some students believe that within their essays there should be a completely discrete section dedicated to the historiography. This is clumsy and will detract from your argument. If you consider that historiography is a form of evidence, then the principle of using it should be the same. Integrate it. If it is a separate section it is not supporting your argument in a sophisticated way. Instead, the examiner will see your argument as separate and may miss the connections between your thesis and your understanding of the historiography. Integrating it demonstrates the connections without any doubt and can also offer interesting perspectives and counter-arguments, which provide balance and awareness of the implications of the different approaches to the issues and events.

The key is to drip the historiography into your essay. If you have a pertinent quotation or interpretation, build it into the paragraph much like I explained you should do with the evidence. A neat way to think about this is that the evidence supports your thesis, and the historiography supports your use and choice of evidence. In other words: I am arguing x, y shows why, and z is an authority that bears this out. Building your paragraphs up like this is a logical and rhetorical technique, which will leave the examiner, once again, nodding and ticking and confident in your writing.

There is an interesting relationship between evidence and interpretation, which can sometimes be confusing in terms of historiography. Indeed, sometimes the two overlap. Let's consider the phrase we used in the last chapter: 'It all began with bread.' I explained how this was an excellent piece of evidence as it encapsulated the social and economic causes of the February revolution and as it fitted in with the student's thesis that this uprising was popular in comparison with what happened in October.

However, looking more closely at the phrase (and it remains undoubtedly a piece of valuable evidence), we can see that it reveals an interpretation of the events leading to the uprising. Figes, with this short sentence, demonstrates his own priority in classifying the causes. He shows us that, ultimately, hunger and socio-economic desperation were important motivating factors. The words 'It all began…' imply there are other factors – the politicization of the middle classes, disillusionment with the war, Nicholas' increasing isolation – but that the lack of bread was the significant, short-term starting point. This then is an interpretation: he seems to identify a social and economic problem as the fundamental issue above the political changes that had occurred in the fifty years or so previous, without discounting these. In effect, he places an immediate problem – no food – in context: disillusionment with the Tsarist system, the growth of political opposition, and a desire to leave the war. When you use historians' ideas then, you must always be aware that on the one hand they are pieces of evidence, but on the other there is often a sense that this 'evidence' goes hand in hand with an interpretation. If you drip your selected evidence and this kind of historiography into your paragraphs, you will achieve the same effect: your argument will be fully rounded, coherent, balanced and sophisticated. It will be analytical.

The mark scheme also makes specific reference to the circumstances that lead to differing interpretations, i.e. why might historians disagree beyond different interpretations of the available evidence? Here there is a sense of political historiography and context, the most obvious being, perhaps, the Soviet/Revisionist debates. But this is a tricky requirement. There will not necessarily be straightforward reasons for diverging opinions other than on an interpretive level: not all periods and topics will contain the political or ideological perspective to allow that. Equally, you are writing within the confines of a 50 minute exam essay, and discussing a particular historian's background – as you might do a source in Paper One or the Coursework component: origin, purpose, value, limitation – is not practical. You have neither the time nor the space. This then, answers my quibble regarding the word 'may' discussed earlier.

'May' means 'where relevant'. If your topic does have a number of approaches, it is often the case that there are clear reasons for them. But don't worry about finding them if they don't exist or are not defined enough to allow a discussion. In an essay on the First World War, for example, including Lenin's idea that it was essentially capitalist and imperialist (Imperialism as the highest form of Capitalism [sic]) is worthwhile as you can then connect this to his specific ideology. Equally, Hosbawm's basic, Marxist assertion that the war was caused by the capitalist system and not an individual country fits in with this politico-historical tradition. However, as a contrast, an assessment of Alexander II is based principally on the reforms, the impact and his assassination: a historian's personal politics is perhaps less relevant.

An interesting example is to consider Nazi Germany and specifically the weak/strong dictator scenario and the Final Solution. Here, an essay will need to address in some detail both the Intentionalist (essentially that Hitler's intentions can be traced back to the 1920's and that there was a straight line from this to Nazi policy) and Structuralist (that the nature of the Third Reich enabled much of this policy outside of Hitler, though his intentions are not disputed) positions. Both positions have heavyweight advocates and both draw on considerable evidence in their formulation. One way to drip in the ideas is to maintain a thematic structure, put forward the connecting thesis, and then include how the evidence adds to either or both positions at the end of the paragraph, thus showing both understanding that there are two distinct schools of thought, and also an awareness of the implications of addressing this topic.

Before we look at an example from an essay, let me just give you one thing not to do. There is a yellow IB endorsed book – 20th Century World History: Course Companion – in which there is an excellent overview of the origins of the First World War. Within this section, there is a page that outlines five historians' opinions, from the very famous – Fischer, Hobsbawn, Ferguson – to the less well known – Fay, Stoessinger. This book is produced under the IB and it would be tempting for a student (or teacher) on reading this page to think that a good essay on the causes of WW1 might be structured around these opinions. Or, indeed, that a large discrete section might be devoted to it. **Avoid both of these ideas at all costs**. When there are a large number of interpretations, it is best to stick to the few that are relevant in terms of supporting your thesis, or acting as a counter argument. While historiography is an important component of a successful essay, in the same way that evidence should not become narrative, it must not dominate. Like a good teacher, historiography should support and encourage, but not dictate. The activity that the book outlines, however, is extremely useful and will provide a decent framework for dripping the differing opinions into your essays.

Now, let's have a look at an example paragraph and see how it can be done answering the following question:

'The nature of Tsarist rule from 1881-1914 was dominated by a balancing act of liberal need and autocratic desire.' Assess the validity of this statement.

This extract is from the paragraph addressing the political policies of the Tsars and how they balanced with Russian necessity.

Politically, both the Tsars were characteristically defensive of their autocratic rights, rejecting liberalizing and democratizing Russian forces to exercise and protect their power. Alexander III introduction of "Land Captains" was an extension of the safeguard system, which ensured that centrally appointed delegates could interfere with local government reforms and affairs. This seriously diminished the power and political potency of Zemstvo and dumii around Russia. This apparently autocratic move has however, been debate among some Russian historians, like Thomas S. Person, who claim that the introduction of land captains has been seen as a measure indicating Alexander's desire to maintain his autocratic power, but was in fact an answer to the widespread abuse of power by peasant officials after the introduction of the Zemstvos. Although possible that Alexander's message was a reaction to liberal

reform, it was in no doubt a move that cemented his commitment to maintain traditional Autocracy.

The use of historiography here demonstrates that the student is aware of the debate that surrounds this question of intention: was Alexander's decision simply due to a desire to cement further his autocratic position, or was there an element of sorting out the theoretically 'democratic' Zemstvo and therefore at least connected to liberal reform, if not a liberalising move itself?

Referencing the debate as he has done, there is also the sense of supporting the thesis and yet providing balance, as I discussed above. By introducing the debate, the student shows that essentially the Tsar's *were* 'characteristically defensive of their autocratic rights', while demonstrating to the examiner that he understands the implications of the question and the tricky idea of intention to maintain autocracy, yet prevent adverse reaction from below.

Naming a specific historian too certainly helps.

Here is a further example, part of a response to the question:

'Lenin's ultimate goal was the creation of a single-party Bolshevik state.' Assess the validity of this statement

It is taken from the section on Economics. The student's thesis demonstrates Lenin's willingness to be flexible as regards ideology:

The New Economic Policy was designed to garner popular support for the Bolsheviks after disastrous War Communism. It allowed, and encouraged, an active form of low-level free-market capitalism. Liberal historiography, especially that of Richard Pipes, has been somewhat limited in its explanation of the both the NEP and War Communism: instead of seeing their wider implications, rabidly anti-communist literature has attempted to the use the two to prove that Communist economic models are doomed to fail. As Revisionist Orlando Figes points out, this is indeed a limited view: both the Economic policies were wider exercises to gain and consolidate single-party Bolshevik power, opportunistic and hopeful rather than ideologically motivated.

Note here the positioning of the historiography: the student classifies the historians by school and demonstrates how their political/ideological preoccupations dictate their interpretations of these economic models, thus hitting all aspects of the top mark band as regards historiography referenced above.

Let's now look at another full essay.

'The nature of Tsarist rule from 1881-1914 was dominated by a balancing act of liberal need and autocratic desire.' Assess the validity of this statement.

An examination of Tsarist rule form 1881 to 1914, characterized by the rule by two of the most conservative Tsars in Russian history, reveals that far from a "a balancing act", the two ignored calls and needs for progressive liberalization in Russia and instead focused solely on their desire to maintain autocracy. [*Establishes thesis*] This thesis can be examined by looking broadly at the social, political and economic policies of the respective Tsars, and how these balanced with balanced with Russian necessities. [*Thematic structure plus specific detail and awareness of the implications of the question*]

Social policy under both Alexander III and Nicholas the II are indicative of the autocratic focus of both rulers, and how this autocratic focus meant that the needs and desires of the populous were largely ignored; this does not mean however, that Russia's people did not eventually reap their revenge. Under the guidance of Pobedonostsev Alexander the III was encouraged to roll back the liberal social reforms his father had introduced. The Loris-Meliokov proposals that aimed to create a consultative body for the Tsar were flatly rejected even though, as historian Hans Heilbronner describes in vivid detail, there was resounding support for them amongst important members of Alexander II's administration, such as Valuev and Milyutin. [*Historiography here supports thesis and critical commentary – and is integrated effectively*] They all stressed the need to complete the liberal actions of Alexander II's early years in power, claiming that the reform schedule had become half-hearted and that Russia needed to create liberal social bodies that would help to ensure both her progress and the survival of the Autocracy. Alexander III listened to neither; his own belief in the power of his Tsar, confirmed by the assassination of his father meant he refused to give Russia the liberalizing social reform it needed. In August of 1881, Alexander III went further, reversing the liberal measured set in place by his father with by introducing the "Safeguard System", a series of governmental instructions which in case of "emergency" gave the state police extraordinary repressive powers; ignoring that the assassination of his father in Russia was an indication that his liberal reforms had lagged behind necessary change. The policy of Russification under Alexander III, a broad policy encompassing the ideas of autocracy, orthodoxy and Russian nationalism, further demonstrated his social repression. [*Excellent use of evidence to support and develop the thesis*] Far from realizing that the national dynamics of Russia could not be seen as homogenous (implying by its nature a need for a liberal and open-minded approach), Alexander III approached the empire as a place to be shaped to his desires and needs. His inability to consider Russia's liberal need only further created disillusion among his people, creating the extraordinary social anger that would characterize Nicholas II's reign.

Nicholas's reign **[*Note comparative structure within the thematic structure, offering an excellent technique to perform an analytical comparison*]** was characterized, particularly after the 1905 revolution, by forms of social repression to maintain autocratic power, rejecting the liberal reform that his country clearly needed. After the 1905 Revolution, from early 1906, Tsarist forces indulged in brutal floggings, torture, execution and rape to attempt to reintroduce order into the countryside. Far from realising that peasant starvation and revolt was an indication of the necessity for liberal change, Nicholas remained deluded in the belief that through force he could maintain his autocratic power. Nicholas' necessity to liberalize was not just brought about by the workers or the peasants; there was significant middle class support in Russia for a moderation in Nicholas' rule. By following a policy which painted him as a repressive ruler, determined at all costs to ensure autocracy's continuation, Nicholas alienated liberal minded middle class Russians, a decision which would cost him dearly later on in his reign, when his social support would dwindle to almost nothing. **[*Demonstrates understanding of historical processes*]** From the introduction of the Duma system in 1905, Nicholas also failed at any point to acknowledge the need for liberal reform. He continue a repressive set of measure up until the war, characterized by act of extraordinary violence: the Lena Goldfield massacre on the 17th of April 1912, in which some 270 peasants were executed just for asking for reduced daily hours. Nicholas' policies then, betray a leader who was obsessed with exercising his Autocratic power, even if it was at the cost of morality and social support. **[*Links to introduction and thesis*]**

Politically, both the Tsars were characteristically defensive of their autocratic rights, rejecting liberalizing and democratizing Russian forces to exercise and protect their power. Alexander III introduction of "Land Captains" was an extension of the safeguard system, which ensured that centrally appointed delegates could interfere with local government reforms and affairs. This seriously diminished the power and political potency of Zemstvo and dumii around Russia. This apparently autocratic move has however, been debate among some Russian historians, like Thomas S. Person, who claim that the introduction of land captains has been seen as a measure indicating Alexander's desire to maintain his autocratic power, but was in fact an answer to the widespread abuse of power by peasant officials after the introduction of the Zemstvos. [*Effective demonstration of historiography and why there are differing views*] Although possible that Alexander's message was a reaction to liberal reform, it was in no doubt a move that cemented his commitment to maintain traditional Autocracy. The issuing in 1881 of the State Powers Statute only emphasizes Alexander's desire to exercise his autocratic power to crush political opposition. Liberal judges who might be light on revolutionaries were removed and replaced with harsher special courts designed to maximize punishments. In the press, the statute ensured that reporting was highly controlled, and the reporting of state difficulties or political problems was strictly forbidden. In 1887, the University statute created similar conditions: radical student unions were crushed and entries made more strict to ensure that politically dangerous people could not join. Alexander's policies then, demonstrate that he was a ruler ignoring the reality of the nation around him – diverse, politically active and changing – by imposing autocratic rule instead of balancing this against liberal need.

Similarly, [*Good comparison*] Nicholas II could not reconcile the need for political liberalism with his desire to maintain total power. The Introduction of the Fundamental Laws in March of 1906 however, appeared to be a moment where Nicholas was accepting the need for gradual liberalism. With the introduction of a state Duma, it seemed like Nicholas was taking the steps after the 1905 revolution to create a more politically modern Russia. However, the treatment of the Duma by himself and Stolypin between 1905 and 1914, demonstrated that by its third dissolution and re-convocation, it had become purely a political instrument to allow the Tsar to retain his total political control. The moves which Nicholas needed to make to ensure his political survival in Russia, the genuinely politically liberal compromises, were never actually acted upon. That the Duma's first set of requests to the Tsar was for the liberation of imprisoned revolutionaries further exemplifies Nicholas' dedication to maintain autocratic power. Far from a policy of rapprochement, after 1905, Nicholas had sought to retain the gains in terms of political repression that he had made in 1905. Unwilling to work with the Duma, Nicholas proved to those around him that only with a full scale revolution could genuine reform be instated. Ironically, Nicholas' inability to foresee that his autocratic desire and inability to make liberal compromise would create the political class that would eventually kill him and his family and end The Romanov dynasty. [*This paragraph builds on the opening thesis very well, integrating evidence and critical commentary and concludes with a good sense of historical context and processes*]

Alexander III economic policies demonstrated his hope that liberal need could be bypassed to maintain a strong grip on autocratic rule. [*High level of conceptual thinking and establishes the thesis*] Alexander wished to encourage internal economic growth after the disastrous Crimean War in 1853, to ensure that Russia as an Autocratic, imperial power retained its influence. The work of both Bunge and Vyshnegradsky, was supposed to create a rapid phase of industrialization characterized by little or no social reaction. However, this industrialization led to the famines of 1891 and 1892, proving once again the need for a shift into more co-operative economic reforms. Even though he had been presented with the failure of an economic system that places Tsarist power above all else, Alexander still refused to adopt genuinely liberal and progressive economic reform. The construct of railways under Sergei Witte, although an extraordinary exercise in modernization, did not address the fundamental problems which underlay Russia's economic problems. Alexander failed to realise that successful economic policy would consolidate his power through gradual reform; instead, his obsession with the strengthening of Russia's military position ensured that Russia's fundamental economic problems went unsolved. *[Good overview and excellent level of detail in this paragraph]*

Nicholas demonstrated in his economic policies a similar *[Further comparison]* desire to ensure that liberal reform could be bypassed to consolidate his rule. Instead of tackling the wider problem, addressable through liberal reform, Nicholas chose to target a few, attempting to create a set of conservative peasants, diving the Russian peasantry into a class divisions. His policy was however, badly directed and politically ineffective. Although Stolypin recognised the need to create economically independent peasants, Nicholas' fundamental conservatism never allowed him to fully complete this economic objectives. The Tsar's inability to accept liberalising reform, his unmoving belief that any ground lost was a violation of god's will meant that the economic situation in Russia deteriorated to a point where both workers and peasants were suffering greatly.

In conclusion, Neither Alexander the III not Nicholas the II balanced liberal need and autocratic desire: both instead indulged in the second, which would bring about their degradation politically socially and economically. Socially, Alexander the III's inability to recognise the need for liberal reform lead to an exercise in the consolidation of autocratic power which disillusioned large sectors of society hoping for greater liberalisation like that of Alexander II. Similarly, Nicholas' seconds repression after the 1905 revolution failed to recognise that the Russian people had demanded a change. Instead, he used repression, exercising political power, but essentially destroying his own public support. Politically, Alexander III embraced open repression and "counter-reforms" against those set in place by his father. Nicholas instead, used the semblance of liberal reform to exercise autocratic power in the form of the Duma, ending any later chance for political compromise. [*This is an excellent comparison, succinct and perceptive. The conclusion really doesn't need much more*] Finally, the economic policies of the two revolved around the creation of a powerful Russia without subjecting her to social unrest; the success of their attempts played out in February of 1917.

Chapter Six – The allusive style and the benefits of counterfactual thinking

The allusive style

"The Allusive style is perhaps the end point of the Safe Hands approach. It is not something that exists independent of the other elements in this book.

" I found that Joe described my writing as 'allusive' towards the end of our time working together. This was because the allusive style was the culmination of a growing appreciation of how to create an essay around a thesis, structuring it in a logical and analytic way, appreciating the difference between narration and analysis, using varied evidence in a balanced way and incorporating historiography well into the essay.

"It is then, hopefully at least, the end point of the tools outlined in the book, and where, if I was sharp and focused, I could arrive to in my own essays using them."

This last chapter covers possibly the least concrete of the aspects of the Safe Hands approach and is something of a culmination of all of them. They relate to the overall style of your essays and the way you might approach them in order to ensure that you address all of the implications of the questions.

So, what is 'the allusive style'?

When writing essays, you are distilling – hopefully – a mere fraction of your knowledge on a topic, taking certain aspects of evidence and interpretation and marrying them to a thematic structure that will frame and support your argument. I have discussed before the daunting weight of the Higher Level syllabus, and, often, exam questions will focus on very specific aspects encouraging you to explore the debates and not simply write down everything you know about a period. Essentially, one of the principles of good exposition is to only include what is pertinent, either as supporting or counter argument. Examiners do not want to see vast swathes of connected but irrelevant narrative.

However, it also important that you demonstrate that your essay is indeed something of a distillation and that you have drawn your ideas from a deep reservoir of knowledge accrued over the course of your study. They need to feel that they are in Safe Hands – that you know what you are talking about and that you have made active decisions about what to include and what to omit and for valid reasons. In a sense, you need to *appear* hugely knowledgeable, whether, in fact, you are or not. (Of course, the best way to appear to be hugely knowledgeable is to actually *be* hugely knowledgeable.)

How to do this?

Here's where 'the allusive style' comes in.

To allude means to refer, to suggest, to imply, to mention without expounding on at length. Much in the same way that you need to use evidence to support your ideas without descending into narrative, with the allusive style, you should be demonstrating breadth of knowledge through reference and suggestion, and depth through analysis.

There are several ways to do this. You must ensure that you use appropriate terminology (writing on Nazi Germany, for example, and making sure you spell Volksgemeinschaft and Gleichschaltung correctly); you need to mix the 'types' of evidence I discussed in an earlier chapter – doing so provides a rounded and balanced piece of writing. Essays that have as their evidence base only dates and statistics or anecdotes or historians' views, will feel limited. A range of types of source will demonstrate variety in your own reading and research.

Another significant factor in the allusive style is confidence. Confidence in your writing is not the same thing as belligerence in argument. Indeed, the best and most confident essays are balanced and consider counter-arguments: the confidence comes through in the willingness to concede that there are other ideas worthy of discussion. No, confidence is about the examiner feeling in Safe Hands. The structure and details of the preceding chapters should help instil confidence. Just like appearing to be knowledgeable is easier when you are knowledgeable, confidence is a difficult thing to fake. Another word might be 'accomplished'. Jeffrey Eugenides once told a writing class of his that when writing fiction you should imagine you are writing a letter to your smartest friend, that way you will never dumb down nor explain what is unnecessary. I think that writing a History essay is not that dissimilar. You should imagine you are writing to your smartest friend, but one who knows little about History beyond general knowledge. The explanations you provide in your essays should be analytical – your smart friend will know the basic chronology. Try, if you possibly can, to think of examiners as smart friends (though there are teachers all over the world who will consider examiners neither smart nor friendly).

(As a little aside – and relevant to sixth-formers in a very different way to essay writing – I just read this in a newly published novel, The Unknowns by Gabriel Roth: '…knowing that confidence is valuable doesn't help you acquire it – it just pushes your confidence toward the closest extreme. Confident people know they have an advantage and become more confident; insecure people know they have a handicap and become less confident.' Now Roth's narrator is talking about courtship, though it's not only true for getting girls or boys to like you. The point is that the Safe Hands approach for essay writing will boost your confidence through its secure framework and thus enable that extra confidence that this advantage will bring – the extra assurance and authority that *being* confident brings.)

There is another way to build and demonstrate confidence: **only write what is one hundred percent true**. That might sound odd given as we do not really know. But think about what this means. It is about style. It is about using words such as 'perhaps' or 'suggests' or 'implies'. Using those words (and others like them) make everything one hundred percent true. Often, a student will make a statement that may be too bold or too forthright. Usually, with a little tweaking, the same statement will work beautifully in an argument. As you practice this approach and adopt this allusive style, read back your work and ask the question: is this one hundred percent true? If it's not, remember this: History is a subject that encourages debate, that is dynamic and changing and that is all about interpretation. Then, stick in a word like 'believe' or 'appear' or some other conditional, and the sentence will work.

Here's an example of my own:

While there was a clear escalation in policy and violence against the Jewish population in the 1930's, it is arguable that this was a premeditated escalation in terms of actual policy. The Intentionalist school offers Mein Kampf and the 25 Points as indications that Hitler and the Nazi leadership were prepared to follow an explicitly anti-Semitic campaign, including the Nuremberg Laws and culminating, domestically at least, in Kristallnacht. However, the Structuralists – while accepting this overarching intention – demonstrate that the policy-making was piecemeal and opportunistic.

Here, the key word is in the first sentence: 'arguable'. The second important 'allusive' element is the referencing of evidence ('Mein Kampf and the 25 points') and the concise overview of the historiography.

Consider this as a comparison:

There was a clear escalation in policy and violence against the Jewish population in the 1930's and it was a premeditated escalation in terms of actual policy. The Intentionalist school offers Mein Kampf and the 25 Points as indications that Hitler and the Nazi leadership were prepared to follow an explicitly anti-Semitic campaign, including the Nuremberg Laws and culminating, domestically at least, in

Kritallnacht. However, the Structuralists – while accepting this overarching intention – demonstrate that the policy-making was piecemeal and opportunistic.

While there doesn't seem to be much difference between the two examples, the second very clearly nails its colours to the mast: the student seems to be falling very much on the Intentionalist side with little regard to the Structuralist argument. The first sentence is the key:

There was a clear escalation in policy and violence against the Jewish population in the 1930's and it was a premeditated escalation in terms of actual policy.

Yes, there was an escalation: one hundred percent true. Yes, it was premeditated in the sense of the inherent anti-Semitism of the National Socialists: one hundred percent true. But is it one hundred percent true that this premeditation was 'in terms of actual policy'? I.e. did the Nazi party have a map drawn up of what they would do, specifically? Now, it can be argued, yes. But the Structuralists suggest otherwise. So this final part of the sentence is **NOT one hundred percent true**, as there are established and valid arguments that exist to counter it. That's what I mean. Use 'arguable' and you show awareness and appreciation of the debate and the implications of a related question. This emits confidence.

Building your essay on the Safe Hands approach will give it a sound foundation, which in turn breeds confidence. Constructing each paragraph on a thesis-development-evidence-historiography model, leads the examiner through the steps he wishes to see as reflected in the mark scheme. Peppering your essay with a range and variety of types of evidence provides an insight into the depth of your reading and understanding. And finally, practice. Use the approach, but bang those essays out: confidence comes from repetition and incremental progress. But once you get the knack – and I guarantee that you will – you will never, ever lose it.

The benefits of counterfactual thinking

"I always had a problem with counterfactual conjecture in my essays. I would regularly claim that "if x hadn't happened then surely…". I enjoyed writing these, but they were not the stuff great history essays are made of. I am no Nostradamus.

"Joe used my natural narrative, counterfactual instinct as a tool to help me think about <u>what did happen</u>, ultimately as a way of making me observe historical situations for what they were. The way of thinking outlined in the following chapter helped me to pad out my essays using the thought process, but not allowing the conjecture to enter into the essays themselves."

(First, a caveat: the following illuminating anecdote comes from about fifteen years ago. Not only can I not recall the exact words or order of events but neither am I completely sure that I am representing the two eminent professors as I should be. Oh well. It doesn't really matter – the point is that I have this memory and it affected me and frankly that is the most important thing. Is it 'evidence'? Is this a 'historical fact' now I have written it down? Why don't you ponder those questions after you've sat your exams?)

When at university, I attended a series of lectures by Niall Ferguson on Russia. They were excellent. At around the same time, he had just published, as editor and contributor, a book called Virtual History, which is a series of essays based on the 'what if...?' premise, or Counterfactual History. At the same time I was studying eighteenth century England under the mighty Professor Paul Langford, author of A Polite and Commercial People. During a tutorial, I remember making a counterfactual remark along the lines of 'well, if that hadn't happened, then the face of constitutional monarchy may have been very different!' Langford sighed and explained to me the – obvious, really – idea about each event being singularly unique, a deterministic idea I discussed earlier. He then made a disparaging remark about new-fangled ideas of rewriting the past. (There was something of a journalistic trend, I think, of which Langford disapproved.)

I was slightly conflicted. I respected Ferguson hugely and enjoyed reading his section of the book. I also found the idea to be at least an amusing one, even if not really a 'historical' one. But while I respected Ferguson, I actively *feared* Langford so decided that counterfactual thinking (and especially counterfactual publishing) was a waste of time. 'Don't speculate!' became a constant refrain in my lessons. 'Only write what is one hundred percent true!'

However, recently I have decided that there are benefits to counterfactual **thinking,** though I still stand by my 'Don't speculate!' mantra in written work. So what are these benefits? Well, firstly, I have recently understood that my own mistake was not necessarily an error in thinking, but in expression. Sometimes, causation can be understood more clearly if we consider what **didn't** happen. Doing that helps us realise the significance of what did. But, it's no good expressing it this way – 'imagine if x hadn't happened, then y would have been different'. This is naïve, faulty reasoning and entirely inappropriate for a History essay.

But counterfactual thinking can help you appreciate the **precariousness** of History. So much hangs on so little, it sometimes feels to me. (Again, this is naïve, but interesting…) Think about the long-term socio-economic currents versus the Great Man idea I alluded to (see what I did there?) earlier. Broad trends culminate in individual action, which create change or consequence. And these individual actions seem sometimes to occur on a whim, or an inspired guess. Think about the October Revolution: Lenin was unconvinced the time was right. It was Trotsky that persuaded him. Who knows how he did it, exactly? Perhaps he used a particular word or phrase that he knew Lenin would respond to? Perhaps Lenin was hungry and simply lost the will to disagree? Ok then, if it'll shut you up and let me eat, let's do it! Or perhaps Lenin knew deep down that the time *was* right but needed an accomplice to reassure him?

These speculative sentences are utterly worthless in academic terms. But they are interesting. And they raise a counterfactual question, which may help you to understand Russia in 1917 a little better. What if the Bolsheviks hadn't acted? What would have become of the Provisional Government? Now, I'm not going to answer the questions, but I will say this: the proliferation of political parties, the problems of the Dual Power, and the worsening economic and social problems as caused by continued involvement in the First World War means that the future was anything but certain. Imagining what didn't happen can sometimes help you realise why what did happen, did. The unique process of causation, or: if something is different to what it is, then it is something else. Brilliant.

117

Just don't ever write it in an essay. It is a thought-experiment. It is to explore ideas and causes in the mind. 'History is the study of causes' remember. On the page: only write what is one hundred percent true.

Now, an example paragraph from this question:

'Lenin's ultimate goal was the creation of a single-party Bolshevik state.' Assess the validity of this statement

This paragraph is from the political section.

Lenin's political policies between 1917 and 1920 betray the reality of his abandonment of ideology in favour of ensuring that the Bolsheviks were able to remain the only party in Russian politics. The failure of the Bolsheviks in the November 25th, 1917 Constituent Assembly Elections, and Lenin's subsequent dissolution of the assembly demonstrate the contempt he had both for Russian democracy and even his own purported ideology. Lenin and the Bolshevik party as a whole had relied on a promise for democratic change to garner meagre popular support at the height of Provisional Government unpopularity: after all "All Power to the Soviets" was a statement which demanded that the only "revolutionary" and "democratic" body in Russia be given power. The scenes at the Tauride Palace however, were representative of the reality of how the Bolsheviks had both gained, and would create a single party state: Red Guard soldiers, getting drunker and drunker, aimed their guns at SR speakers to amuse themselves from the Palace's gallery – this was power consolidation by intimidation and force, not by democracy. When Lenin had believed that the elections would consolidate Bolshevik power, and legitimize the elimination of political opposition, he was happy to hold them. When they failed, he ensured that Military power and force ensured that the Bolsheviks were the only party with political power. In essence, the Civil War (1917-1922) was an extension of these conflicts, the final great battle to make Russia Bolshevik. Of course, Marxist historiography from the this period has centred around the need to fight the "Counter Revolution", an abstract idea that Lenin also used to dissolve the constituent assembly as well as engage in Civil War. However, both Liberal and Revisionist views share common features in their interpretation of political policy and action between 1917 and 1924: they were almost inevitably exercise towards the creation of a single party Bolshevik state irrespective of both ideology and popular political belief. This is undoubtedly the most compelling view. With the dissolution of the constituent assembly as the most compelling example of Bolshevik rejection of their own ideology, the Civil War, as well as rejection of any democratic negotiation with rival parties, all demonstrate Lenin's desire for a single, all powerful, political party.

The paragraph holds a steady position without lacking in balance; there is a terrific mixture of types of evidence (dates, statistics, anecdotes, historians); there is a considered approach to the historiography and an attempt to explain why the different schools of thought exist. The paragraph is a decent example of the allusive style and is born of confidence and practice. The student who wrote all the essays in this book wrote a whole lot more. With the principles and the practice, paragraphs like this one will come naturally and assuredly.

Let's now have a look at the whole essay.

'Lenin's ultimate goal was the creation of a single-party Bolshevik state.' Assess the validity of this statement.

A question regarding what Lenin's ultimate goals were as leader of the Bolshevik party rests on one of the great ideological debates of the past century. [*A little dramatic perhaps, but does get to the essence of the consequences of Lenin's creation...*] Was Lenin's true goal the creation of genuine, powerful communist state, or was his main aim the consolidation of Bolshevik power to the point where there was no plausible political opposition? [*Pertinent question – framing it like this shows the examiner the heart of the debate*] Assessments of Lenin's motivations behind policies to consolidate power in this period have been of great historiography debate, [*Perhaps a brief indication of 'why' here would help*] which frames the arguments of this essay. Broadly, an analysis of political, economic and social changes under the Bolsheviks allows for the most genuine assessment of whether or not Lenin's primary desire was the creation of a Bolshevik state.

Lenin's political policies between 1917 and 1920 betray the reality of his abandonment of ideology in favour of ensuring that the Bolsheviks were able to remain the only party in Russian politics. [*Develops the thesis*] The failure of the Bolsheviks in the November 25th, 1917 Constituent Assembly Elections, and Lenin's subsequent dissolution of the assembly demonstrate the contempt he had both for Russian democracy and even his own purported ideology. Lenin and the Bolshevik party as a whole had relied on a promise for democratic change to garner meagre popular support at the height of Provisional Government unpopularity: after all "All Power to the Soviets" was a statement which demanded that the only "revolutionary" and "democratic" body in Russia be given power. The scenes at the Tauride Palace however, were representative of the reality of how the Bolsheviks had both gained, and would create a single party state: Red Guard soldiers, getting drunker and drunker, aimed their guns at SR speakers to amuse themselves from the Palace's gallery – this was power consolidation by intimidation and force, not by democracy. When Lenin had believed that the elections would consolidate Bolshevik power, and legitimize the elimination of political opposition, he was happy to hold them. When they failed, he ensured that Military power and force ensured that the Bolsheviks were the only party with political power. In essence, the Civil War (1917-1922) was an extension of these conflicts, the final great battle to make Russia Bolshevik. *[Recognises significance]* Of course, Marxist historiography *[Appreciation of historiography and the reasons for it]* from the this period has centred around the need to fight the "Counter Revolution", an abstract idea that Lenin also used to dissolve the constituent assembly as well as engage in Civil War. However, both Liberal and Revisionist *[Develops historiography and effectively integrating it]* views share common features in their interpretation of political policy and action between 1917 and 1924: they were almost inevitably exercise towards the creation of a single party Bolshevik state irrespective of both ideology and popular political belief. This is undoubtedly *[This word is too strong and may alienate an examiner]* the most compelling view. With the dissolution of the constituent assembly as the most compelling example *[Here, however, the student shows a good sense of priority]* of Bolshevik rejection of their own ideology, the Civil War, as well as rejection

121

of any democratic negotiation with rival parties, all demonstrate Lenin's desire for a single, all powerful, political party.

Lenin's economic policies between 1917 and 1924, demonstrate only further how Bolshevik ideology and policies could be moulded and twisted to suit the needs of power consolidation: from the strictest form of economic communism ever practiced in Russian history with War Communism, Lenin abandoned Leninist-Marxist economic ideology to consolidate his power with the NEP. [*Develops thesis and identifies key content, which in turn shows an analytical approach by connecting the evidence with the themes*] To consider War communism simply an economic policy, would be to seriously underestimate its political and social potential. Obsessed with the 19th century revolutionary Paris communes, Lenin believed that the economic threat posed by the peasantry was the only factor that threatened his control both economically and politically. War Communism then, was a two-fold policy, designed to consolidate Russia's economic power while ensuring dominance over the Peasants. It hoped to starve the peasants and feed the workers, destroying a "counter-revolutionary" threat while ensuring that the proletariat remained contented. This was not however, a policy designed with the welfare of the people in mind, it was an economic necessity in a time of war which threatened the Bolshevik state. The fact that it failed, with both the peasantry and the proletariat left starving for long periods during the civil war, brought about the NEP, the most blatant rejection of Marxist-Leninist economic ideology. [*This is strongly worded, but here, I think, an examiner will like the bold statement as it is not controversial and it shows an understanding of political ideology*] The New Economic Policy was designed to garner popular support for the Bolsheviks after disastrous War Communism. It allowed, and encouraged, an active form of low-level free-market capitalism. Liberal historiography, especially that of Richard Pipes, has been somewhat limited in its explanation of the both the NEP and War Communism: instead of seeing their wider implications, rabidly anti-communist literature has attempted to the use the two to prove that Communist economic models are doomed to fail. As Revisionist Orlando Figes points out, this is indeed a limited view: both the Economic policies were wider exercises to gain and consolidate single-party Bolshevik power, opportunistic and hopeful rather than ideologically motivated. [*Excellent integration and overview of the historiography – detailed without dominating*]

Socially, the repression of the Red Terror as well as the peasantry during War Communism demonstrates that far from fulfilling genuine ideological or Communist goals, Lenin ensured the consolidation of Bolshevik power through a continuation (and perhaps exaggeration) of some Tsarist forms of political repression: [*Effective connection with the past and thus revealing a good understanding of context and processes*] Flaubert had once said "in every revolutionary there is hidden a Gendarme", never was this more true than during the Red Terror. [*Slightly pretentious, but nice to see, I think…*] Unsurprisingly, Marxist historiography [*Good sense of the provenance of historiography*] has relied on the supposition that Lenin was fighting an "internal civil-war" against the bourgeois counter-revolution. However, the random nature of the Red Terror and the levels of sadistic violence involved, demonstrate that it was in fact an extraordinarily brutal form of social limbo, a way of ensuring that both fear and violence stopped any popular opposition to the Bolshevik state. It is no surprise that in this period, the Cheka, the Bolsheviks state police, soon became known as the "*oprichniki*", the name given to their old Tsarist counterparts. Far from a policy of selective political counter-revolutionary purging, the Cheka's arrests were appallingly random. People were imprisoned purely because of their name, the belonging they had in their pockets, and even minor social misdemeanours such as cue jumping. As one railway worker

123

from Kozlov put it "Red is the colour of truth and justice, but under the Bolsheviks it has become the colour of blood". This was exactly it, the Bolshevik leaders had long left behind the principles and ideals they had supposedly carried with them during the revolution. Revisionist historians argue that the Red Terror was a pragmatic policy, used during the civil war to ensure that there was not enough organized popular anger to threaten the Bolsheviks. [*Contrast*] This is probably the most convincing interpretation: Lenin proved once again, that far from wanting to establish a genuinely communist or socialist Russian state, terror was an instrument to ensure and confirm Bolshevik power. [*Fits with the evidence integrated into the paragraph*]

In conclusion, it seems hard to deny that indeed Lenin's ultimate goal was the creation of a single party Bolshevik state. Although idealized Marxist interpretations of the Russian revolution claim that Lenin's social, economic and political moves were to protect Russian revolution and socialism, rather than the Bolsheviks themselves, this view is undoubtedly limited. So too however, are liberal interpretation of Lenin's policies as proof of the inevitably violent consequences of communism. Instead, revisionist views offer the most balanced and reasonable explanations: [*Referring to the historiography again is effective here as it frames the essay and was explicitly outlined in the introduction as a key aspect*] Lenin's policies and actions were pragmatic decisions in all spheres of Russian life, designed to ensure that his party was able to consolidate power, and make Russia into a single party state.

Chapter seven – A word on Paper Two

Up to now we have focused on essay questions that are based on a Paper Three topic. As I said at the beginning of the book, the distinction between the papers is fairly irrelevant when it comes to writing your essays. I stand by that. And it is worth emphasising.

Paper Two topics do have broad comparative themes – for the Single-Party States topic, for example, you have the origins, consolidation and policies of the totalitarian state. A question may ask you to compare one state with another within one of these specific themes. This comparative exercise will be one you will have done in class – looking at the different ways in which a totalitarian state is set up or examining how different states use different models to maintain power. But in terms of essay writing, even in a comparative format, the principles are the same.

There is a broader sense of change and movement in the Paper Two topics, apparently. But look at the Paper Three Russia topic that we have been focusing on. The change is more than considerable. It is massively broad! Over fifty years of radical shifts in politics! The Third Reich only lasted twelve. (Of course that is not to understate its impact, only to give a sense of perspective in terms of time.)

Equally, Paper Three requires more depth of focus. But how can that be right when examining Hitler's Germany in Paper Two? It is a condensed twelve years with enormous political, social and economic policy change and includes the Second World War. If that doesn't require at least the same level of depth, well…

In the introduction I mentioned the mark schemes of the two papers: they are almost identical in what they define as a successful essay. The Safe Hands approach builds the structure and techniques that will achieve success, no matter in which exam you are writing.

Let's have a look at a Paper Two style question to demonstrate this. You'll see the Safe Hands approach is equally effective.

Assess the significance of Lenin's economic policies between 1917 and 1924.

To assess the significance of Lenin's economic policies between 1917 and 1924 is also to assess the successes and failure of those policies, their economic impact, and their political weight. It is however, very difficult to quantify and qualify the true effects, successes and failures of Lenin's economic policies, as debate between historians is still ongoing today. There are however, three broad politico-historiographical schools regarding the Lenin's policies: Soviet and Marxist interpretation, the Liberal school, and revisionist historians. Bearing in mind these historiographical differences, Lenin's two major policies "War Communism" and the "New Economic Policy" can be assessed in terms of their economic, social and political significance.

Socially, both War Communism and the NEP showed Bolshevik willingness to put down what they perceived to be social threat to their regime: War communism represented a "war" not only economically, but against possibly dangerous peasants, while the NEP was a concession when the oppressive measures introduced by the Bolsheviks threatened to create a peasant revolution. Although Soviet historians have argued that War communism and its effect on the peasantry were in fact part of Marxist ideology, a revisionist view of the Bolsheviks paints them as primarily concerned with possible social revolution. The requisition of grain and the nationalization of industry, the ban of private trade, where all a way to ensure that the populace could not rise against the Bolsheviks at a time when they were weakened by the civil war. This ushered in the era of "The Red Terror", a measure that ensured that although weak, the Bolsheviks would still be feared. The Cheka formed in 1917 as Russia's first revolutionary "Security State Organization", captured and imprisoned, often without reason or evidence, hundreds of thousands of people. Many were tortured, some finding themselves captured just because they shared a name with a known "counter-revolutionary". The primary social effect of war communism was mass disillusionment: ordinary Russians no longer believed that the Bolsheviks represented the revolution; they had become like the oppressive "*oprichniki*", the hated Tsarist secret policy. Along with this social unrest, the peasants, suffering most during the period of war communism, began to revolt, at some points putting Lenin and the Bolsheviks under serious and sustained social pressure.

The NEP was a response to this social pressure, and proved the effect that social factors could have the Bolshevik's own handling of economic policy. The peasant uprisings and the problems War Communism had caused where clear to Lenin, and he was fully aware that a continuation of these revolts could develop into full-scale social revolution. The retreat that Lenin implement was not ideological, as soviet historians have claimed: instead it was a pragmatic economic decision to quell social unrest. The relaxation on forms of capitalism was an evident step forward, a thawing in the Bolshevik's relationship to the peasants. The NEP however, although popular with many Russians, was a stunning blow to old school Bolshevik workers who quickly named the policy the "New Exploitation of the Proletariat". The rise of NEP men, traders who flourished in get-rich-quick property speculation and trading, embodied the social discontent caused among many of the workers by the NEP: vulgar, uncouth and flash, the NEP men were the embodiment of the kind of capitalism the Bolshevik's had claimed to be destroying. The general effect of the Nep was however, to produce a period of economic growth, coupled with a quieting of revolt, generally helping to create a grater social clam.

Politically, the significance Lenin's two major economic policies are ironically opposite: War Communism was the first and last time that true non-free market economics would be adopted, while the NEP was the embracing of a capitalist economic model. That is not to say however, that outside of the ideological factors that make up their political significance, their value as policies to help retain political power should be overlooked. Neither Soviet historians, who have seen War Communism as the great embrace of communist ideology, a moment where Lenin's promises to truly fulfill a Marxist revolution were realized, nor Liberal and Revisionist descriptions of the policy as a pragmatic political move are entirely convincing. Orlando Figes in his seminal work "The People's Tragedy" argues that adopt either is to ignore a fundamental fact about what War Communism meant. He argues that the true significance of War Communism in that it proved once and for all that the Bolsheviks were not willing, and never would be willing, to co-operate or share power in Russia. The terror then, marked a moment of real political significance: as members of the Left SRs, Mensheviks and Kadets sat in the Peter and Paul fortress, they must have wondered in 1918, at how the revolutionaries had so quickly become the oppressive Tsars. This "internal front" had a political significance in that it also confirmed the Bolshevik's war against the peasantry, once again seemingly conforming to traditional Marxist ideology, once again confirming that even if it was only adopted for pragmatic economic and social reasons, the decision to adopt War Communism was in itself and endorsement of Marxist ideology.

It is partially for this reason that the adoption of the NEP was such a politically and ideologically devastating blow to traditional communists. For Trotsky, the party's most outspoken advocate of War Communism's continuation, the NEP was a betrayal. Ideologically, it was totally contrary to both Marxist and traditional Bolshevik interpretations of economic policy. As well as appeasing peasants, a group that Marx had doomed to "extinction" in his theory of "historical development", Lenin argued that in a country dominated by Bourgeois, there would have to be a period in which socialism was established alongside the free market. Bukharin called it a "temporary retreat", but the political significance of the NEP lies not in its abandonment of Marxism, but what that abandonment said about Bolshevism: that it was an ideology geared to the maintenance of power, at whatever cost, even the fundamental ideological and political principles that underlay its own ideology. Liberal and Revisionist historians have pointed to this fallacy as the most telling political development of the 1920s, particularly more reactionary liberals, who argue that the NEP was the final and conclusive example of Lenin's political ideology being one of oppression and pragmatism, based not on political ideals, but a constant struggle for the maintenance of power.

An economic evaluation of the significance of War Communism and the NEP points to War Communism as a failure: an economic policy designed to feed the cities and starve the countryside, it only starved the cities further and turned the country-side against the Bolsheviks. The NEP too, the adoption of large scale free-market acceptance was not an economic success; although raising the Russian economy as a whole, it failed to meet ideological aims of improving worker living standards. War Communism, in essence a socio-economic war against the peasantry, failed to meet its target of greater grain for the cities and starvation of the country. To look at the statistics of the years directly following the introduction of War communism, is to quantify its failure on both counts. By 1920, small factories in Petrograd were producing 43% of their 1913 total, even more devastating, large factories just 18%. The lack of food, caused by the failure of the Bolsheviks to effectively requisition grain, and the peasants' desire to hide, keep or burn any excess grain, ensured that far from feeding the workers, by 1920, they were starved and unhappy. The average Moscow worker had a productivity rate of 44% less than the

130

1913 figure. The struggle for food also cost many Bolshevik workers their jobs. The attack on the peasantry, and paranoia that grain was going to be requisitioned, meant that much of Russia's arable land was focused on the growth of food. This meant that there was an 87% drop in the number of acres given over to cotton. Hundreds of Russian cotton manufactures closed down, being deprived of their most basic resource. It seems then, that War Communism did little but ensure that peasants starved, that workers starved and lost their jobs, and that the Russian economy stagnated. Lenin's experiment into true Marxism had been an utter failure.

The NEP was at least statistically a success. Outputs from 1921 and 1925 improved steadily. The grain harvest in 1921 was 37.6 million rising by a massive 72.5% in 1925. Coal output rose form 8.8 million to 18.1 million tons in 1925. Average wages of workers went up to 25.2 from 10.2 rubles between 1921 and 1925. Yet its significance was more than that. Although there was an economic recovery, and a clear move towards a more successfully controlled free-market economy, the NEP failed to really improve the standard of living for the workers. It did create economic opportunity for more enterprising peasants and of course created the new class of NEP men, yet it had at its heart a fundamental failure. In terms of expected Bolshevik ideology, and socialist belief in general, the economic significance of the NEP was that it proved that although economics in general terms could be related to improvement of the Russian economy, this would not meeting Bolshevism's own criteria of improving the living standard for the workers themselves.

In conclusion, by looking at broad differences in the political, social and economic significances of Lenin's two major economic policies, it is clear that both represented incredibly important shifts in all three areas of though. War Communism, in essence a social war against the peasantry proved economically disastrous. This compounded the problematic political reality of the policy: it was the first real implementation of full scale economic Marxism, and its failure was a terrible indictment of Bolshevik ideology. The NEP social and political significance are intimately tied. Politically, the NEP was a violent departure away from traditional Marxist ideology, and this had the social impact of disillusioning many workers who felt like the principles they had supported the Bolsheviks for were fast disappearing. Economically too, the NEP exposed the fallacy of the free market: although helping Russia to recover economically, the NEP set up the conditions the Bolsheviks had promised to fight, keeping static the conditions of the vast majority of workers, while opportunist businessman gorged themselves on the luxuries of speculation and capital.

Reading List:

The following books were all invaluable in the writing of the sample essays, Historical Investigation and other revision essays not included here.

- Carr, E. H – 'The Twenty Years Crisis'
- Clarke, Christopher – 'The Sleepwalkers'
- Clark, Martin – 'Profiles in Power: Mussolini'
- Collier, Martin; Rees, Rosemary – 'Heinemann Advanced History: Hitler and the Nazi State'
- Figes, Orlando – 'A People's Tragedy'
- Figes, Orlando – 'Natasha's Dance'
- Figes, Orlando – 'Whispers: Private Life in Stalin's Russia'
- Graham, Helen – 'The Spanish Civil War: A Very Short Introduction'
- Howard, Michael – 'The First World War: A Very Short Introduction'
- Kershaw, Ian – 'Profiles in Power: Hitler'
- Phillips, Steve – 'Heinemann Advanced History: Stalinist Russia'
- Smith, S. A. – 'The Russian Revolution: A Very Short Introduction'

Acknowledgements

Firstly, I would like to thank my mother for her unfailing patience and love during the last 4 months of my IB. Without her I would not have been able to write these essays.

I would also like to thank Crispin Germanos, for instilling in me a love for the writing of history at school; my father for showing me that history could be fun from a young age; Anurag Jain for his support and help in times of personal and intellectual difficulty; my sister as a constant source of love and backing; and Sarah May Maguire for her careful reading, support and advice while I was writing my introductions.

Finally, I would like to thank Joe for giving me the tools to accomplish one of my major educational goals. I hope that the passion and love he has for teaching, his subject, as well as the humor and fun of his lessons, will be brought across in this collaboration!

Lorenzo Brewer

Lightning Source UK Ltd.
Milton Keynes UK
UKOW01f1856141014

240099UK00007B/568/P